RICHMOND BEER

A HISTORY OF BREWING IN THE RIVER CITY

LEE GRAVES

Photography by Jennifer Pullinger | Foreword by Mark A. Thompson

AMERICAN PALATE

Published by American Palate
A Division of The History Press
Charleston, SC 29403
www.historypress.net

Front cover skyline image courtesy of Rich Terrell of http://www.richterrell.com/.

First published 2014
Second printing 2015

ISBN 978-1-5402-1011-1

Library of Congress Cataloging-in-Publication Data

Graves, Lee, 1948- 0eauthor.
Richmond beer : a craft history of brewing in the River City / Lee Graves.
pages cm. -- (American palate)
ISBN 978-1-5402-1011-1
1. Beer--Virginia--Richmond--History. I. Title.
TP573.U6G72 2014
663'.4209755451--dc23
2014035307

CONTENTS

FOREWORD

W hat a long strange trip it's been. The brewing industry has gone from boom to bust to boom again, and this book covers the whole story in the capital city of the commonwealth of Virginia. The history of beer is a fascinating one that many believe is part of the reason we have civilization as we know it today. Once beer was discovered, it made more sense to settle down, grow grain and not go foraging for nutritional sustenance. But I digress.

As a native of Charlottesville, I was reminded in the opening chapters of this book of the importance of our founding fathers in the journey of beer. Thomas Jefferson's home, Monticello, is a place where our third president and governor of Virginia brewed copious amounts of beer. Jefferson publically declared, "I have lately become a brewer," and in some ways, this was the beginning of the first boom of beer in America.

My personal path into the world of beer began in the early 1990s. After reading Chapter 6 of this book, I was reminded of how long and strange my trip has been. I was born and raised in Charlottesville, Virginia, before heading out to Portland, Oregon, in 1990 with a bachelor of science degree from James Madison University. Little did I know at the time, but when a good friend came to visit from Virginia, it would change my life forever.

My friend's name was Jamie Zobel, and we grew up together in Charlottesville. Jamie came to Portland to attend the 1992 or 1993 Craft Brewers Conference. He persuaded me to tag along with him to check out what was, at that time, a fringe movement in America. At that point in my life, I had very little interest in "microbrewing," as it was called then (now

FOREWORD

it's called craft brewing). About two years later, in 1995, Jamie returned to Richmond, Virginia, to start the James River Brewing Company. The brewery lasted only a couple of years, and as this book rightly points out, making great beer is very different from making money doing so.

A few years after Jamie's visit, I began my professional brewing career in Portland with a now-defunct brewery called Nor'Wester Brewing Company. From Portland in the early 1990s, I went to Denver, Colorado, to work at Mile High Brewing Company in the mid-1990s and eventually returned to my hometown of Charlottesville in 1999 to found Starr Hill Brewery.

Lee Graves's book covers the history of beer and brewing in Richmond, Virginia. He writes about the founding of Virginia and the importance of beer as nutritional sustenance that helped a young nation survive—how the Native Americans helped teach the English settlers how to make a "corn" beer due to the lack of raw ingredients. The book also covers the "great experiment" of Prohibition, which nearly wiped out the brewing industry.

The section of this book that I could not put down deals with the beer revolution that is happening today. This great revival is chronicled with amazing detail and shows how Richmond went from three breweries in the late 1990s (Legend, Richbrau and Main Street), down to one or two through most of the 2000s and now boasts upward of thirteen breweries.

Lee Graves and I first met in late 1999, just a couple of months after I opened Starr Hill in Charlottesville. In those formative days of craft brewing in Virginia, you could count the number of breweries in the state on two hands, and there were few people writing about beer at the time. Lee was known as "the Beer Guy" (and still is), and he wrote a regular column for the *Richmond Times-Dispatch*. The band of brothers in 1999 was very small, and I think we all gravitated toward other like-minded people like Lee. We have remained close friends for going on fifteen years, and his passion for craft beer and talent as a writer are on full display in this book. Whether you are a history buff or have come recently to the craft beer scene, this is a great read that covers Richmond's brewing world from the beginning. I highly encourage you to sit back, grab a fresh Virginia craft beer and enjoy this book.

Cheers,
MARK A. THOMPSON
Founder, Starr Hill Brewery
Chairman, Virginia Craft Brewers Guild

ACKNOWLEDGEMENTS

T his book would not have been possible without the patience, support and expert editing of my wife, Marggie. She's the best there is, no question.

I also owe a huge debt to my best friend (aka Beer Buddy), Les Strachan. He has been at my side through many adventures, from a Glasgow bar in his native Scotland to the convention floor of the Great American Beer Festival in Denver, and I attribute my love of beer to his sharing his own passion many years ago. My daughters, Helen Marie and Cassie, also have been inspirations and sidekicks; they appreciate the value of a perfect pour.

I want to acknowledge the folks at The History Press, particularly Banks Smither, for keeping me on the path to completion. Smither's quick responses and caring approach have meant tons. My collaborations with photographer Jennifer Pullinger and artist Kristy Heilenday could not have been more enjoyable and productive.

I smile to think of Starr Hill Brewery's Mark Thompson and his willingness to write the foreword. We go back such a long way; our friendship has been a treasure.

A tip of the hat, as well, to Mary Garner-Mitchell for helping with images and to Robert Powell, editor of *Virginia Business* magazine, for sharing his love of history and his expert editorial eye.

On the newspaper side of things, the *Richmond Times-Dispatch*, a place I called home for many years, has helped with images and other support. Since the early days of my "Beer Guy" column, the editors and photographers on

ACKNOWLEDGEMENTS

the *T-D* staff have been thoughtful and responsive. A special salute goes to librarian Heather Moon.

The research for this book was expedited considerably by organizations and individuals in Richmond's history community: the Virginia Historical Society, particularly Jamison Davis; the Valentine Richmond History Center, particularly Kelly Kerner; the Library of Virginia, particularly Carl Childs; the Richmond Public Library; and the National Park Service, particularly beer history lovers Mike Gorman and Eric Mink.

I think I wore out the Internet researching stuff on the Library of Congress's Chronicling America site. Searching through those old newspapers might have tested my eyesight, but it yielded some great stories.

One particular resource was invaluable—*Richmond Beers: A Directory of the Breweries and Bottlers of Richmond, Virginia*, by Danny Morris and Jeff Johnson. I can only hope that I have added a brick or two to the foundation they have created.

Members of the Peter Stumpf family also have been gracious and helpful. Chip Stumpf let Jennifer and me into his home to check out the Stumpf memorabilia and take photographs.

On a national level, the Brewers Association, based in Boulder, Colorado, has been an invaluable resource for data about craft brewing and trends in the industry. Staff economist Bart Watson was particularly helpful in parsing out information about Virginia, and Julia Herz, craft beer program director, became an instant friend to all who met her during a 2014 visit.

I will always remember an afternoon spent in Colonial Williamsburg with Frank Clark, supervisor of Historic Foodways and one of Virginia's great beer and food historians. I and several other beer lovers quizzed him extensively while he was putting together a colonial ale, and his knowledge, wisdom and humor made for a lively episode.

Last, and certainly not least, the RVA beer community—what can I say? The support, help, encouragement, friendship and downright love that I have received from Richmond's professional brewers, homebrewers, brewery owners, brewery owners' wives, brewery reps, distributors, beer lovers, beer officers, beer historians, beer writers and beer readers leave me forever grateful. One bunch I'd like to thank in particular—folks who don't get enough attention—are the people behind the bar at Mekong Restaurant, Capital Ale House and RVA's many other fine restaurants and taphouses.

Thanks to all!

INTRODUCTION

S ometimes things come together in the strangest, most wonderful ways. I had just saddled up the "Beer Guy" column for the *Richmond Times-Dispatch* after a hiatus of a few years when I received an e-mail from The History Press asking if I might be interested in doing a book about Richmond beer.

Beer? Richmond? History? Beer? Twist my arm a little harder.

Frankly, I was as much intimidated as excited by the prospect. For Virginians, history is no idle pastime. Jamestown, Powhatan, founding fathers, mother of presidents, Civil War, civil rights, civil wrongs—the state looms large in the nation's identity. Richmond has a central role in that drama, and any project attempting to focus on one facet of that history must look through multiple lenses.

Thus it is with beer. I had only the faintest inkling at first, but I quickly came to understand that the story of beer reflects the story of Richmond itself. From beer accompanying English colonists to the falls of the James River in 1607 to a brewery adjoining a Civil War hospital in Chimborazo, from German lager earning kudos upon its arrival in the mid-1800s to Hardywood Park's Gingerbread Stout receiving a perfect rating from a prominent beer magazine and from beer being stored in riverfront caves to beer flowing from tasting room taps—Richmond has always loved, embraced and celebrated beer.

What I could not have foreseen is that the project would coincide with a renaissance on several fronts—brewing, dining, artistic creativity, urban hipness, outdoor recreation and civic pride. *Frommer's* mentioned the craft beer and restaurant scene in recommending Richmond as a top tourist destination in 2014. Mekong Restaurant on West Broad Street was repeatedly named America's best beer bar in voting on craftbeer.com. *BeerAdvocate* magazine rated Richmond highly after brother-founders Jason and Todd Alström visited several local breweries and Mekong. As this book was going to press, Stone Brewing Company of California named Richmond among three finalists for a regional facility. The list goes on.

Since I started researching this book, more than half a dozen breweries have opened in Richmond. One of my great pleasures has been getting to know the owners, brewers and beer lovers associated with each operation and tracking how they have fit into both the craft-brewing circle and the larger community. With this book, I hope to illustrate how the current picture is part of a broader canvas, one filled with stories of people and their passions dating to the country's beginnings.

One of my buddies who is a professional historian urged me to use his characterization of Richmond's beer history as one of booms and busts. I prefer to view it more as an ebb and flow, similar to the river that courses through the heart of the city. I cannot paddle, or even view, the James River without feeling humbled by its beauty and power. So it is when I contemplate the forces of history and the possibilities of the future. Indeed, many rivers flow through Richmond, and the story of beer is but one.

1
THE FOUNDING BREWERS

The band of explorers sailed upriver from Jamestown in 1607 with great expectations. They had arrived from England only ten days earlier and were eager to fulfill a primary directive of their mission: to find a link to the South Sea. Riches would be their reward, for the Orient was a promised land of gold and other treasures.

For their trip up the James River, the group—five gentlemen, four marines and fourteen sailors led by Captain Christopher Newport—carried only the necessary supplies: food, weapons, items for trade, brandy and wine.

And beer. Or "beere," as Gabriel Archer, chief chronicler of the expedition, spelled it.

This provision proved handy when the travelers landed near a village of Powhatans on a hill overlooking the river. Beer helped break the ice. In one of the first recorded Anglo-Powhatan parties in the Old Dominion, the English and the natives feasted and drank amid cavorting and dancing. They partied a little too hard, it seems, for the combination of "beere, Aquavitae [brandy] and sack [wine]" left Parahunt, son of the powerful Chief Powhatan, feeling "very sick." Newport assured him that he would feel better after sleeping it off. When this proved true, Newport achieved status as a medicine man and was bombarded with questions about aches and pains, according to Archer. The "sleep it off" line went only so far.

And the English discovered they could go only so far. When they finally reached the falls of the James River, they found a roiling cascade that prevented further travel. They planted a cross bearing the inscription

In 1607, English settlers who had only recently arrived at Jamestown shared "beere," brandy and wine with Powhatans at the future site of Richmond. *Illustration by Kristy Heilenday.*

"Jacobus Rex, 1607," gave a great shout and, after deluding the Powhatans into thinking they really weren't claiming the land for King James, departed downstream.

More than a century would pass before Richmond would take shape as a city, but much of its course was framed in that encounter. The mighty James River remains a defining element in the flow of events that have made Richmond one of the most historic cities in the nation. And just as beer was there at the beginning, it has continued to play a role in the region's story.

A Necessary Item

Beer, in fact, was necessary for survival in 1607. The colonists came from a culture where water, fouled from centuries of sewage, was unfit for drinking. Beer, which required the water to be boiled, became the drink of the masses. Low-alcohol versions—small beer and table beer, as they were called—resulted from a technique common among brewers at the time. They used the same grains for repeated mashings, like using the same coffee grounds for multiple brews. Each run resulted in beer that was less potent and more suited for simple thirst quenching.

In the New World, particularly in swampy Jamestown, that habit of avoiding the water continued, sustaining the need for beer. Jamestowners realized they had made a drastic error in not having a brewer among the first wave of settlers.

"Faced with the growing frustration of the colonists [at the lack of beer], the governor, Sir Francis Wyatt, approved an advertisement in England for two brewers to make the crossing. So eagerly was the arrival of brewers anticipated that one of the first crops planted in the settlement was barley," writes beer historian Gregg Smith.

Necessity spurred improvisation. In 1620, Captain George Thorpe observed that his fellow colonists, prompted by a shortage of ale, "found a way to make a good drink from Indian corn, which he preferred to good English beer," Smith says.

Today's drinkers might have found the brews of the 1600s hard to swallow. Beer was dark and cloudy; it was very much like the ales that had been brewed for centuries. "Despite its foul appearance, people knew beer was good for them; indeed, it was a major part of their diet and continued to be so throughout America's early years," Smith says.

Early settlers used a variety of ingredients and simple methods to brew beer, as demonstrated during a program at Colonial Williamsburg. *Photo by Lee Graves.*

This recipe for spruce beer uses porter as a base and to supply the yeast for fermentation. *Charlotte County (Va.) Salt Distribution Register, 1862–64. Local government records collection, Charlotte County Court Records, the Library of Virginia.*

Virginia's colonists found the climate too warm for large-scale commercial brewing, but domestic kitchens routinely bubbled with ale and porter. Women, as always, occupied a central role in brewing, and recipes ranged widely. Persimmons, sassafras, pumpkin, cornstalks, spruce needles, molasses and a host of other ingredients found their way into brew kettles—along with the usual hops and barley. Yeast still was a mysterious agent, so brewers were careful to propagate their yeast cultures from batch to batch.

The founding fathers loved their ales and porters. During his stays in Philadelphia, George Washington developed a particular passion for the porters of the Robert Hare Brewery, which he imbibed regularly between sessions of the First and Second Continental Congresses. Thomas Jefferson kept ale, as well as wine, at his table and investigated the potential for establishing a national brewery, largely to combat the rampant drunkenness fueled by rum and whiskey. Martha Jefferson, his daughter, cultivated quite a reputation for her ale in the region around Monticello. Records show her paying for seven pounds of hops with an old shirt. (Now there's a great name for a beer: Old Shirt Pale Ale.)

TAVERNS AT THE HUB OF LIFE

Just as beer occupied a familiar spot at the dining table, it also played a leading role in the life of taverns. Ordinaries, as many were called, and inns existed not just as watering holes or spots for pub grub; they also held a central place in colonial life. Men debated politics, judges held court sessions, travelers shared news—many even shared beds—all with mugs of ale and cider in hand.

Taverns were so ubiquitous, in fact, that two existed in Richmond before William Mayo and James Wood began formally plotting the city in 1737. By that time, William Byrd and his son, William Byrd II, had built the area into somewhat of a hub for frontier commerce. The Byrds, with thousands of acres at their disposal, recognized the value of the river as a highway for trade, and the forbidding falls continued to focus attention on the hills and plains around the James as fertile turf for homes and businesses. Mills crushed grain into flour, barges carried coal downriver, slaves toiled and the river periodically roiled. At the point where Shockoe Creek emptied into the James, a small community named Shaccos emerged with a tobacco warehouse that was designated an official inspection station. The village

The pleasure of your company is requested at the **BALL,** *at the EAGLE HOTEL, to be given in honor of* **GENERAL LA FAYETTE.**

	MANAGERS.	
JOHN MARSHALL,		ANDREW STEVENSON,
ROBERT POLLARD,		JAQUELINE B. HARVIE,
JAMES GIBBON,		ROBERT G. SCOTT,
JOHN BROCKENBROUGH,		BERNARD PEYTON,
WILLIAM H. CABELL,		WILLIAM LAMBERT,
JOHN COALTER,		TEMPLE GWATHMEY,
BENJ. WATKINS LEIGH,		THOMAS N. PAGE,
JOHN ROBERTSON,		JOHN G. WILLIAMS,
PHILIP N. NICHOLAS,		THOMAS GREEN,
THOMAS RITCHIE,		WYNDHAM ROBERTSON,
PETER V. DANIEL,		JAMES LYONS, JR.

Richmond, October 15, 1824.

Taverns and some hotels were centers for daily affairs as well as special occasions, such as this ball at the Eagle Hotel honoring General Lafayette in 1824. *Virginia Historical Society.*

became a commercial center with a store, a ferry, a chapel and more. Byrd was building a small empire and was reluctant to surrender control by establishing a municipality, but the Virginia General Assembly forced his hand and required that a town be established. Richmond became a legal entity in 1742. Population: 250.

So when Mayo and Wood drew up their thirty-two squares, each with four numbered lots, in the areas we now know as Church Hill, Shockoe Bottom and Broad, Main, Cary and Canal Streets, taverns already existed. One was at Cary and Twenty-third Streets, where Richard Levens kept an ordinary in his home; the other was at Main and Twenty-third, where Abraham Cowley did likewise.

More inns quickly mushroomed. Imagine, if you will, a walk back in time, ducking into taverns of yesteryear on today's streets. Start at the Eagle Tavern, on the south side of Main between Twelfth and Thirteenth Streets. Opened in 1787, it was a rectangular frame building with an open court in the middle. The preliminary hearing for Aaron Burr was held there before his trial for treason in 1807. In 1824, Richmond "had the greatest civic and social affair in her history" in welcoming the Marquis de Lafayette; festivities included a ball at the Eagle.

Continue east a few steps to Richard Hogg's Tavern, also known as the Old Tavern, on the southwest corner of Main and Fifteenth Streets. One of the more popular spots, it created some buzz in December 1781, when Hogg and three other Richmonders, including fellow publican Gabriel Galt, were arrested and charged with disloyalty by the British army for their activity in helping the rebel cause. They never stood trial.

Also at Fifteenth and Main, you would find Bowler's Ordinary, another frame building. Though the ordinary stood six feet above street level, the river still occasionally found its way in, as the delightful memoirist Samuel Mordecai observed in his 1860 book: "An old citizen who died some years ago said that he had paddled a canoe into Bowler's Tavern—and a living one tells me he has crossed the street there in a boat."

Bowler's was supplanted by the Bell, where General Lafayette and General George Washington were entertained in 1784, after the Revolutionary War was won.

Still continuing east, you'd pass Formicola's Tavern to get to Galt's, on the northwest corner of Main and Nineteenth Streets. When Benedict Arnold raided Richmond in 1781, Galt's became his headquarters, but then it also served Cornwallis and Lafayette. One officer in the Continental army wrote of enjoying an evening of billiards there and dining "very sumptuously upon Rock fish."

The pub crawl continues east to Cowley's, one of the two originals, and the illustrious Bird in Hand, another of the oldest taverns in the city, on the northwest corner of Main and Twenty-fifth Streets. The list goes on—Rocketts Landing Tavern by the docks; the Swan on Broad between Eighth and Ninth; Richard's Tavern just west on Broad; Baker's Tavern on Brook Avenue; and the Neapolitan, where John Marshall, who later became chief justice of the United States, met with his club members while starting his legal practice in 1781.

Smaller taverns dotted the city. The Rising Sun, on Fourteenth Street south of Main, was famed for its beer, as well as its owners, Caspar Fleisher and his wife. "The rotundity of Caspar and his wife gave warranty that their table was well served and their beer not small, for beer was a general and genteel beverage in those days," Mordecai recalled.

Perhaps the Fleishers brewed their own beer, as some tavern owners did. Regardless, demand was huge. "Great quantities of beer were drunk, including both the strong beers which were imported from England, such as Bristol beer, and the small beers which were produced locally. Cider and rum were also popular and were served in all of the taverns," records a history of taverns.

Brewery Saved by a Widow

The first records of brewing in the Richmond area focus on the banks of the James to the south and to the west. On December 8, 1777, John Mayo of Manchester advertised in the *Virginia Gazette* that he was "intending to set up a brewery and distillery at this place. I have provided two stills and three coppers, one of which contains about 300 gallons." Mayo dangled the opportunity for the right person to become a partner in the enterprise. But I couldn't find any records, stories or anecdotes of the existence of an actual brewery.

More details tell the tale of Westham Foundry, about six miles upriver from the city. As the Revolutionary War raged, Virginia's fathers commissioned building a foundry to make and bore cannon barrels using coal from Chesterfield and iron ore brought from the hinterlands. The receipt book of Colonel Turner Southall, who supervised the foundry, carries numerous entries from 1778 documenting expenditures for work on a brewery at Westham. In 1780, the brewery was put up for sale, and records indicate that William Hay teamed with Southall to operate the enterprise, which produced "most of the beer consumed in the city of Richmond."

Richmond succeeded Williamsburg as the state capital in 1780, largely because of Richmond's more central location. Though its tobacco warehouses made it a rich economic plum, Richmond had little strategic significance in the war and escaped conflict until 1781. General Benedict Arnold then brought his forces to bear on the city, sending Governor Thomas Jefferson and others in a scramble to save public records and avoid devastation. Resistance was scant. One of the few skirmishes occurred near the present Strawberry Street in the Fan District, and some say that accounts for the nickname "Scuffletown."

Arnold dispatched troops under Colonel John Graves Simcoe (no relation to me or to the hop) to Westham to destroy the foundry. He and his men wreaked havoc on the ironworks, but the brewery "was saved by the intercession of the widow who owned part of it," wrote Lieutenant William Feltman of the First Pennsylvania Regiment. He came through Westham in August 1781 and saw the "very fine brewery" that had escaped the ravages of "that d---d rascal Arnold."

As one century yielded to another, scant mention of breweries remained. Mordecai wrote, "The Tredegar Iron Works are on the spot where Colonel Harvie erected at the close of the last century a flour mill, a brewery and a distillery. Whether any beer or whiskey was made there I know not."

Scuffletown Tavern stands in one of the few places where General Benedict Arnold met resistance during his 1781 raid, and some sources attribute the "Scuffletown" name to that skirmish. *Virginia Historical Society.*

Also, around 1800, William Hay and a Mr. Forrester opened a Richmond Brewery on the northeast corner of Canal and Fourth Streets. Seven years later, the operation was leased to Richard Whitfield & Company, which produced beer and porter for a city of 5,730 inhabitants.

Decades would pass before another hometown brewery could offer such products to Richmonders.

2
WAR LOOMS, CONSUMES

The first half of the nineteenth century found Richmond flourishing on several fronts—education, tobacco, river trade—and floundering on others. Streets in the 1800s were particularly challenging, as houses weren't numbered, and some streets, such as Main, were only partially paved. The stretch east toward Rocketts Landing was so pocked with deep holes as to make it "disgraceful to civilized society," the *Virginia Patriot* observed.

That changed in 1833, when the Richmond Omnibus Coach Company announced it was ready to provide service from Rocketts Landing along Main Street to Capitol Square. In the decade before the Civil War, Richmond stood out as a manufacturing center. "Richmond was the industrial center of the South and the region's wealthiest city, based on per capita valuation," wrote Virginius Dabney. "It was the nation's, and perhaps the world's, largest manufacturer of tobacco and…perhaps the nation's second largest flour milling center. The city was also the leading coffee port in the country…[and] half of the tobacco grown in Virginia and North Carolina was marketed in the city."

The city's population climbed from 27,570 to 37,910 from 1850 to 1860. Richmond was "the healthiest city of its size in America and perhaps in the world," proclaimed historian John P. Little.

Taverns continued their importance as centers for socializing, entertaining, holding affairs of public import and drinking beer. One of the most illustrious was the Swan, on Broad between Eighth and Ninth Streets. Though it had many celebrated guests, including President

Right: Edgar Allan Poe, a literary giant during his lifetime, spent his last nights in Richmond at the Swan. *Illustration by Kristy Heilenday.*

Below: One of the most illustrious taverns in Richmond was the Swan, which counted President Thomas Jefferson and Edgar Allan Poe among its many celebrated patrons. *Virginia Historical Society.*

21

Thomas Jefferson, its saddest tale relates to Edgar Allan Poe. A literary giant whose life was plagued by debt, melancholy, a weakness for alcohol and feuds with his adoptive father, Poe spent his last nights in Richmond at the Swan. He left a trunk and an umbrella before leaving for Baltimore; he died a few days later, on October 7, 1849. The trunk remains at the Poe Museum in Richmond.

For beer lovers, this was an exciting time in Richmond. The British influence still was broad. In addition to the porters, stouts, Scotch ales and other brews that had been consumed for decades, a new kid arrived on the dock. Four lines at the bottom of a newspaper column in 1853 announced that "11 casks of 'East India Pale Ale,' imported direct from Liverpool," had been received by a local merchant.

Considering the popularity of India Pale Ales today, this notice fascinates me. As most beer geeks know, IPAs evolved from high-alcohol, highly hopped beer brewed to survive—indeed, mature during—the long journey from England to India, where the British had a strong military and civilian presence. The early versions of this palate-puckering beer came from Hodgson's Bow Brewery in London, which initially had a corner on the IPA market. But brewers to the north of London in Burton, which shipped some of its ales out of Liverpool, rose in prominence because of several factors, primarily that the water there was rich in minerals that led to a clearer, brighter beer. As the 1850s passed, ads in Richmond newspapers tracked the rise of IPAs from Allsop and other Burton brewers.

The arrival of IPAs was only a minor sensation, however. By any measure, the greatest influence on beer in prewar Richmond came from a flood of German immigrants. The stream had been building through the early 1800s, and "during several years preceding the Civil War the German element in the state capital accounted for almost 25 percent of the white population," Klaus Wust wrote in *The Virginia Germans*. Many Germans were the original residents of Jackson Ward.

Predictably, breweries accompanied this surge, and with those came traditions of the Fatherland, including songs of Bavaria and the Rhineland. "Out of these lager-inspired renditions grew the Gesang-Verein Virginia, founded in 1852, the city's oldest musical organization." The group, which spells the name Gesangverein now, performs each year at the Richmond Oktoberfest.

LAGERS ON THE RISE

The beer scene featured a mix of beers from northern "come-here" breweries—which provided a flourishing trade for local bottlers such as John Clendening—and hometown breweries, though details are scant concerning the latter. In 1852, newspapers carried ads for the sale of a brewery at Bacon Quarter Branch—now the Carver section of the city. "Fresh summer lager beer" from the Reading Brewery of Pennsylvania was being sold in 1856 from

GREAT UNION LAGER BEER TRIAL!
AT THE NEW MARKET HOTEL,
CORNER OF 6TH AND MARSHALL STREETS,
On MONDAY, the 26th December—to commence
at 10 o'clock. A. M., and close at 3 P M.
SOUTHERN, EASTERN, WESTERN AND
NORTHERN LAGER BEER !
Admission—FIFTY CENTS, which pays for
all the Lager you drink.
You can drink as much LAGER as you please.
COME ALL, DRINK ; and judge which is the
best LAGER. ——
TO THE PUBLIC.
As there is so much competition among the dif-
ferent Lager Beer Brewers, the Proprietors of the
New Market Hotel concluded to arrange this trial
and let the public be the judges. They have spared
no expense in collecting the Lager from the differ-
ent Brewers of the Union, and therefore expect a
good attendance of the consumers and admirers of
this great Institution—
LAGER BEER!
COME ONE ! COME ALL !
MONDAY, THE 26TH OF DECEMBER,
At 10 o'clock, A. M.
SOUTHERN RIGHTS MEN. ATTENTION !
The first LAGER BEER BREWED IN RICH-
MOND will come out, and deserve particular no-
tice of all Southern Rights men.
GAUTER & LOHNERT,
New Market Hotel.
de 24—2t   Corner of 6th and Marshall sts.

This notice in the *Richmond Dispatch* of 1859 touts "the first lager beer brewed in Richmond." *Library of Congress, Chronicling America.*

J.G. Lange's saloon between Broad and Marshall Streets. Records indicate that "Mr. Hoffman's brewery" was located on Second Street, Frederick Kick operated one at No. 298 Broad Street and Erhardt Richter's brewery opened at the corner of Broad and Seventh Streets in 1859. You could buy a dozen quart bottles of lager at Richter's for $1.25 and, if you lived in the country, have them "packed in boxes and delivered to any railroad depot in the city free of charge."

In 1863, the *Richmond Dispatch* reported receiving "from the City Brewery on Seventh Street near Broad a sample of the beer made there. It is fully equal to Northern beer, having strength, softness and a foam equal to cream ale." Two bits says they were drinking a lager.

Compared with ale, lager provided a distinct appeal to beer lovers. Remember talking about how ales were dark, murky and a bit skanky? Advances in brewing technology—such as using coke to stabilize temperatures and having thermometers, hydrometers and other tools available—made ales more appealing and consistent, but lagers were a whole different matter. And Germans were the masters. Even the word *lagern* comes from the German "to store." The style evolved from the custom of storing barrels of brew in mountain caves during warm months. The yeast and any particulate would settle to the bottom; extended conditioning in the caves enhanced this clarifying process. The result: a beautiful golden beer with a dazzling appearance and refreshing crispness. (Keep in mind, though, that all lagers are not light in color; bocks, doppelbocks, dunkels, schwarzbiers and others come from the dark side, and many were available in Richmond during the 1800s.)

With his usual humorous touch, author Samuel Mordecai observed that "lager has raised its head and a strong one it is, as are those of its countrymen. Lager has gone ahead of all other beverages. The number of 'saloons' that bear its name is scarcely exceeded by that of clothing shops, kept also by Germans. They are a valuable acquisition to our city, in many useful trades. They are also our gayest citizens, and enjoy their hours of relaxation."

A different point of view comes from Samuel Phillips Day, an Englishman who visited Richmond just before the Civil War. One senses a certain attitude in his account: "The German population is not liked in Virginia; they seldom associate, and never assimilate, with the regular citizens, and are generally dirty and untidy in their habits. In some parts of Richmond more German than other names appear over the doors, and to judge from the conversation heard on the streets, one might be at a loss as to ascertain whether German or English was the language of the country."

FROM CLOTHIER TO BREWER

Day also remarked that Germans dominated two occupations: owners of saloons and clothing stores. One of those clothiers was J.D. Goodman, who advertised regularly in newspapers before the Civil War. As the 1850s neared an end, however, Goodman's interests changed. On January 1, 1859, he named J.H. Simpson a partner; in ensuing months, Simpson and another man took over the business "by mutual consent."

Goodman's eyes were on brewing. By September 1859, Goodman had closed the books on clothing; on Christmas Eve, the *Daily Dispatch* announced that a new beer was being introduced to Richmond's public: the Southern Rights Lager Beer, "the first beverage of the kind ever brewed in this city."

"We know nothing about 'lager,' never having tasted it; but as people will drink that, or something worse, and as Goodman and Richter, the owners of the Southern Rights Brewery, are citizens of Virginia, we should certainly give that the preference," the *Daily Dispatch* reads.

The "preference" alluded to voting for Southern Rights at a citywide Great Union Lager Beer Trial. It was set for the day after Christmas 1859 at the New Market Hotel, which stood at the corner of Sixth and Marshall Streets. Participants paid fifty cents for all the lager they wanted. "Come all, drink and judge which is the best lager." The trial claimed to present brews from every quadrant of the country, and local pride was at stake. (An interesting note: The trial began at 10:00 a.m. and closed at 3:00 p.m. The city streets must have bubbled with yuletide spirit, and by that point, who cared who won?)

Goodman the brewer was going full bore as the decade turned. In 1860, he was taking orders for lager beer, selling grain for feed (brewers still give or sell spent grain as food for livestock) and advertising to buy barley and hops, which, according to their ad, grew wild on the banks of Virginia's rivers.

The brewery's location? Accounts say Rocketts, which extended west of today's Rocketts Landing, by Haskins' Spring. Soon, the brewery would be associated with nearby Chimborazo Hospital, with caves on the hillside.

The beer? Pardon the effusiveness of yesteryear's journalism in this *Richmond Dispatch* account of January 30, 1860:

> *The Lager Beer Brewery, lately established at Rocketts, by Messrs. Goodman & Company, bids fair to prove entirely successful, because of the superiority of the beer over that of any other brewery known to the imbibers of that peculiar beverage. We never tasted a drop of lager in our life, and*

The Chimborazo Medical Museum, part of the National Park Service Richmond National Battlefield Park, includes mention of the nearby brewery. *Photo by Lee Graves.*

cannot, therefore, speak from experience; but some of our friends, who ought to be judges—if experience in use is worth anything—say that Messrs. G. & Co. have no rivals in their business. Lager is perhaps the most innocent of all stimulants, and as people will drink it, the purest they can get is the least injurious.

Ads boasted a weiss-beer in addition to the traditional lager.

But trouble accompanied Goodman. Earlier that January, a driver illegally had left a team of horses pulling a beer wagon unattended while caring for a customer. The horses spooked and charged down Main Street, in turn alarming another team of horses hitched to an Adams' Express wagon, and soon both were dashing pell-mell through Richmond. The Express horses collided with a carriage, injuring the three passengers and driver. The beer wagon team continued, narrowly missing another carriage with four women before plowing into the back of a coal cart with such force that two mules were knocked over and the cart's driver was initially believed dead. To the relief of all, he was resuscitated.

In June 1860, fire struck the brewery. An incendiary caused a blaze that destroyed the building and contents. "The stock of beer in the lower cellar was rendered useless by the excessive heat, and a large quantity of beer was consumed," the *Richmond Dispatch* reported. The loss was estimated at $10,000 to $12,000; insurance covered $6,000. The proprietors were rebuilding on the same site in July, and records indicate that the "new brewery of Messrs. Goodman and Company" was in operation that fall.

That was not the end of Goodman's hurdles, however. Apparently, the arrangement between him and Erhardt Richter did not work out. Goodman ran a newspaper ad in May 1861—the same month Virginia seceded from the Union—saying Richter had violated the partnership agreement and "left this State for the North." Richter's wife was arrested in June 1861 for suspicion of espionage (she was later released), but she stayed to run a restaurant. Richter and his two sons joined a New York regiment; his sons were killed, and Richter later allegedly went insane.

The record became sparse as war raged. Again in 1861, Goodman advertised to buy hops and barley from anyone who could supply them. A year later, a man looking for the return of a stray cow gave his location as "living on Chimborazo Hill [by] Goodman's brewery." (Trivia alert: Chimborazo gets its name from an inactive volcano in Ecuador, Mount Chimborazo. Definitely material for *Jeopardy!*)

THE MEDICINAL VALUE OF ALE

The Civil War banged on Richmond's door in 1862. As wounded poured into the city during the Seven Days' Battle and other engagements (five railroads converged in the city, bringing casualties from distant fields), Chimborazo Hospital became of primary importance. It was one of the largest, most sophisticated and most efficient facilities of its kind in the Confederacy. Over the course of three and a half years, it would treat roughly seventy-five thousand sick and wounded—more than any other hospital, North or South. The nearby brewery, capable of producing four hundred kegs at a time, had a medical application, for "alcohol in various forms probably was the most popular drug of the times," according to one news account.

A touching story of the restorative powers of porter is found in an 1863 diary entry of Judith McGuire, an Alexandria refugee living in Ashland. She tried to nurse her nephew, who was wounded at Fredericksburg, but efforts failed initially when he could retain neither food nor drink. "In a state bordering on despair, I went out to houses and stores to beg or buy porter; not a bottle was in town. At last, a lady told me that a blockade runner, it was said, had brought ale, and it was at the medical purveyor's." Her brother was dispatched, and he returned with a dozen bottles, which McGuire administered cautiously. "When I found that he retained it, and feebly asked for more, tears of joy and thankfulness ran down my cheeks…Life seemed to return to his system…and I never witnessed anything like the reanimation of the whole man, physical and mental. The hospitals are now supplied with this life-giving beverage… though great care is taken of it, for the supply is limited."

The war's effects on Richmond ran deep, and beer was among the victims. Martial law caused many restaurants to close, and getting deliveries of beer, particularly from previous suppliers in Maryland, Pennsylvania and other points north, became unpredictable at best. That said, beer was being consumed in growing quantities across the nation. According to the *Richmond Whig*, the amount of brew sold in 1860—eight million barrels—skyrocketed to twenty-four million barrels in 1864, "or nearly a barrel apiece for everybody."

Hometown interests did not remain idle, and on the cutting edge of enterprise stood the Euker brothers—Louis, Charles, William and Edward. The four arrived in America from Marburg, Germany, in the 1850s and eventually made their way to Richmond, where they saw opportunities in the beer business. All became involved in the restaurant/saloon business, with Louis Euker & Bro. flourishing as a bottler of lager, ale, porter, Scotch ale, an "XX ale" and cider. It started bottling on Main Street in 1859, bought out a competitor and expanded in April 1861. Edward launched a brewery at Clay and Harrison Streets. The site was across from Buchanan Spring, a source of water for brewing. Keep this spot in mind, for there will be more beer brewed here later.

With the outbreak of war, Louis returned to Prussia. The others, however, joined the Southern cause. William served as a private in a Virginia regiment, acting for a time as a courier in operations around Richmond. Edward had a colorful career, serving as a rifleman initially but joining the cavalry after he had been stabbed and wounded in 1862 by several soldiers in front of his own brewery. For a period, he was the personal courier of General George W.C. Lee, eldest son of Confederate general Robert E. Lee. Charles Euker also served with distinction, rising from a private in the infantry to the rank of colonel after the war.

A HISTORY OF BREWING IN THE RIVER CITY

Louis Euker would return to Richmond after the end of hostilities, but 1865 found the city a smoking shadow of its former self. The first domino of devastation came on April 2, when Robert E. Lee sent word to President Jefferson Davis worshiping at St. Paul's Episcopal Church that nearby Petersburg was about to fall and that Richmond should be evacuated. Citizens fled in droves, soldiers torched tobacco warehouses lest they fall into Federal hands, naval officers blew up their warships, a powder magazine exploded to the north of town, the city arsenal went off like a gigantic bomb, guards abandoned their posts at the penitentiary and hundreds of convicts escaped in a looting spree as flames spread. Many who had not evacuated gathered in Capitol Square, carrying only the barest items of bedding. "Their poor faces were perfect pictures of utter despair. It was a sight that would have melted a heart of stone," wrote the Union general who led troops into the city and extinguished the fire.

On April 4, President Abraham Lincoln made a surprise visit. Plumes of smoke still twirled in the streets, and residents, many freed slaves, thronged to see him. He asked to meet with leading Richmonders, and soon the city was set on a path to transformation.

3
AS RICHMOND REBOUNDS, BEER SURGES

The ravages of the Civil War left a black scar on Richmond. "From the Spotswood [Hotel, at the southeast corner of Eighth and Main Streets] to Fifteenth Street on both sides of Main, through to the canal, is one mass of ruins, burnt, broken and crumbling walls; bricks, mortar, broken granite and bent iron…mortar and broken bricks—erect chimneys and tottering walls," observed a journalist writing for the *Norfolk Post* in June 1865.

Some parts of the city escaped unscathed; residents, however, were impoverished to the point "that money [was] almost a stranger to the pockets of the people." Always a plucky bunch, Richmonders were quick to pick up the pieces. Wooden shanties sprang up where citizens sold lemonade, spruce beer, green apples, sour oranges and molasses candy.

For some, the rubble and ruin represented opportunity. Northerners in particular were quick to invest in rebuilding Richmond, and by October 1865, roughly one hundred buildings were under construction. Beer once again played a fundamental role. The 1866 city directory lists sixteen brewers and bottlers of beer—porter, ale, lager and other styles. Edward Euker's brewery continued at Buchanan Spring. John Deuringer opened the City Spring Brewery on Eighth Street, north of Leigh. And at Rocketts Landing, a five-story facility would rise, putting a lingering stamp on the city and linking it to the nation's oldest brewery.

D.G. Yuengling Jr. grew up amid high expectations. His father, D.G. Sr., emigrated from a small village in the province of Wurttemberg, Germany,

CONTINENTAL BREWERY

TRACY & RUSSELL,
BREWERS of AMBER, PALE, XX, XXX, BURTON, and
East India Ales and Porter,
For Shipping and City Use,
GREENWICH AV., cor. HAMMOND ST. NEW YORK.

The Continental Brewery was one of several "come-here" breweries to surface in Richmond after the Civil War. *1866 Richmond City Directory.*

in 1828. He was eager to ply the craft he had learned in his homeland, and Pottsville, Pennsylvania, proved fertile ground for both his brewery and his family. In 1829, he founded the Eagle Brewery, later renamed D.G. Yuengling and Son.

The eldest of three sons, D.G. Jr. apprenticed at the Pottsville brewery and then went abroad for further training. He was ready to stretch his wings and carry the family flag afield upon his return, and in 1866, he came to Richmond. He was twenty-four, and perhaps because of his youth, the brewing enterprise at Rocketts began as a joint venture with two others—John Frederick Betz, who was D.G. Jr.'s uncle and a

D. G. YUENGLING, JR.   JOHN A. BEYER.

YUENGLING & BEYER,

JAMES RIVER

STEAM BREWERY,

RICHMOND, VA.

Porter, Ale and Lager Beer,

MALT AND HOPS FOR SALE.

The Yuengling enterprise on the James River was in full swing by 1869, when this ad appeared. *1869 Richmond City Directory.*

prominent brewer in his own right, and another brewer, John A. Beyer. It's easy to speculate that Papa Yuengling wanted experienced hands to guide the business. In fact, the property was deeded to D.G. Sr. in 1868, though Junior continued to supervise the operation.

But why Richmond? Certainly the city's rebound promised profits for savvy investors—Rocketts bustled with traffic on its wharves, and there were enough miners in the area to make the coal-country Pennsylvanians feel at home. Another reason, however, might have been at play. According to a pamphlet produced by a company that ended up buying a Yuengling brewery in New York (and might have wanted to pad its appeal), Yuengling had roots in Richmond.

"The original founder was Jans Yuengling, who came to the United States about 1770 and founded his brew tavern in Richmond, Virginia. The original Yuengling ale and lager were famous in the pioneer days of our country. They were the favorite beverages at important social functions

32

throughout Virginia and Maryland," the pamphlet read. That is the sole reference historians have found, however, to Jans Yuengling and Richmond. So, as Mark Noon writes in his book about the brewing clan, "the mystery has yet to be solved."

"Ye Gods, What Nectar Was There!"

Records do show that D.G. Jr. and his partners landed briefly in Richmond's western end, near Buchanan Spring, before building their mega-brewery on eight acres along the James River. It stood some eighty feet high—five stories above ground—and had 196 windows and vaults deep in the earth capable of holding six thousand barrels, according to the *Richmond Whig*. It quoted the building's cost at $200,000, but another source valued it at $79,000. Regardless, it became a community center, with beer gardens and landscaped grounds known as Schuetzen Park (the spelling varies), popular for picnics and shooting outings. It could produce four hundred barrels a day of lager, porter or ale; barley seed and hops were sold as well. Cellars faced south for easy

In addition to its importance as a beer manufacturer, the James River Steam Brewery served as a community center with its Schuetzen Park. *Photo reproduction by Chris Johnson.*

33

access to the river and railroad lines. The use of steam-powered equipment led to the facility's name: James River Steam Brewery.

The beer itself was well received. "Ye gods, what nectar was there!" exclaimed recipients of a Christmas keg at the *Whig*. "Glass after glass was emptied and quaffed with exclamations of satisfaction, and utterances of best wishes for the success of Richmond beer."

Unfortunately, events did not favor long-term success. Though the facility was built to the finest standards of the craft, it followed a traditional model of brewing in cooler weather and storing the beer in the cellars when temperatures rose. The advent of commercial refrigeration, however, allowed other breweries to forgo cellars and ship greater volumes over longer distances with less chance of spoilage. "The extensive cellars of the James River Steam Brewery had become something of an anachronism even during their brief period of use," concludes a 2013 report nominating the cellars for historic designation.

Another blow struck in 1873, one that would eventually wipe out Richmond's hometown breweries. A financial crisis, sparked by overinvestment in railroads, postwar inflation and large trade deficits, led to widespread panic and protracted stagnation. The tough times were a factor in closing four of the five breweries left in Richmond. The steam brewery was the sole survivor by 1878, and it ceased operations the following year; the building was leased to the Richmond Cedar Works, a wood products manufacturer. A fire in 1891 destroyed the brewery building but spared the cellars.

"THEY WON'T DRINK BEER"

By that time, D.G. Yuengling Jr. had moved his attention to breweries in New York. His experience in Virginia seemed to leave a bitter taste in his mouth. "[I] went to Richmond Va., and put $500,000 in a brewery, and came back without a dollar," he told a New York journalist in 1883. "The farmers of Virginia forced their taxes upon the manufacturers, making me pay eighty-five cents a barrel on my beer and admitting distant beers free...The brewery is there yet, idle, and no brewer has been successful in the South. They won't drink beer."

Whoa! Not so fast, Junior. Let's look back at that period. As mentioned, the city directory of 1866 noted sixteen brewers and bottlers. Until the bottom fell out, Richmonders seemed to be thirsty enough to keep three local breweries going—City Spring, James River Steam and Spring Park (Edward Euker's Clay Street brewery with a new name and new partner, Henry Bowler). Louis and William Euker continued with their bottling, offering Bass and Allsop's English pale ales, as well as lager, porter and XXX ale. Francis Dusch's bottling establishment on East Broad Street supplied draught ale, porter and brown stout from Massey, Huston & Company of Philadelphia. Somebody was drinking that beer!

Up on Chimborazo Hill, fate was not so kind to another Pennsylvania brewer. Joseph Bacher arrived in Richmond in 1870 and bought seven acres with the intent of making use of beer cellars on the property left by previous brewers (Goodman among them, I presume). Bacher apparently didn't do sufficient homework. "Because the temperature in the cellar was not low enough to keep the beer, Mr. Bacher's business collapsed in a few years," and he moved back north, said a *Richmond Times-Dispatch* article.

Though there was stillness at Rocketts Landing—and throughout the city's brewing community—after the James River Steam Brewery's closing in 1879, the Yuengling legacy produced one more ripple. George W. Robinson, who was superintendent of the steam brewery, took over the former Euker-Bowler Spring Park site that year and established the Eagle Brewery. Considering that the Pottsville, Pennsylvania brewery started as the Eagle and that its logo makes prominent use of an eagle's image, the name is no surprise. "One of Richmond's rarest brewery bottles is from this brewery, and it is more than coincidence that the trademark eagle perched upon a barrel of 'Premium Lager Beer' mirrored Yuengling's own eagle trademark," writes beer historian Danny Morris. Robinson's Eagle supplied ale and porter to local hotels; the business failed, however, within two years. The Clay Street site would lie fallow for a dozen years, but it would rise again, as would other eagles and hometown beer.

SEMINAL FIGURES ON THE SCENE

To understand the next train of events, let's track the arrival of two seminal figures—Peter Stumpf and Alfred von Nickisch Rosenegk—and set the scene. As the 1880s dawned, Richmond flourished. The population stood at 63,600; it was one of only ten cities in the South with more than 25,000 people. A web of railroads and rows of tobacco warehouses sparked economic growth. City streets rattled with electric trolley cars, "the first commercially successful system of such cars in the world," Virginius Dabney wrote. Organized labor was on the rise, and a morbid scandal played across newspaper pages as stories detailed graves in Oakwood Cemetery being robbed to supply cadavers for medical students.

A native of Germany, Stumpf gained experience in brewing circles before coming to Richmond. Once here, he initially represented Phillip Best Brewing Company, bottling Milwaukee Lager Beer at 1817 East Main Street. Competition was tough—Richmond's directory listed seven bottlers, though not all doing beer, and the market included the likes of IPA from Robert Smith Brewing Company, ale and porter from the Continental Brewing Company and lager from Bergner & Engel (B&E), all of Philadelphia. B&E beers were bottled by our good friend Louis Euker, who offered "special accommodations for ladies" at his Broad Street saloon.

By 1883, Stumpf had added a now-familiar name to his portfolio— Anheuser-Busch and its St. Louis Lager Beer—and a business partner, John Messerschmidt. The beer was a hit not only at Stumpf's address but also at the saloon-restaurant run by his brother Edward at 826 East Main Street. (Another brother, George, worked there as a barkeep.)

Stumpf became increasingly involved in civic affairs, joining clubs ranging from the Elks to the Odd Fellows, and even gained attention for his singing with the Gesangverein-Virginia. Stumpf also excelled as an Anheuser-Busch rep. "It has been said, but not verified, that Peter Stumpf was Anheuser-Busch's first authorized agent on the East Coast," writes Morris. Along with Original Budweiser, the St. Louis brewery offered more than a dozen brands, Faust Beer, Pilsner and Pale Lager among them.

As the decade advanced, the plot thickened. A brewing powerhouse in the making, Robert Portner of Alexandria opened its Richmond branch. Its Tivoli beer went toe to toe with Tannhaeuser, a Bergner & Engel lager. And by 1885, B&E was sporting a new manager in Alfred von Nickisch Rosenegk.

Born in Stettin, Germany, in 1852, Rosenegk was the son of nobles. His father was a colonel in the German army, and at age ten, Rosenegk began his education in a military academy. He served in the Franco-Prussian War and rose to an officer's rank, but in 1875, he severed his military connections and moved with his wife to America. He left behind his life of privilege. "During the first five years of their life in this country the two had to struggle hard for existence...In 1880, he engaged in the hardware business, beginning with a very subordinate position, from which he was gradually promoted," historian Herrmann Schuricht wrote.

Tannhaeuser

UNQUESTIONABLY THE

FINEST LIGHT BEER EXTANT

RICHLY PACKED FOR FAMILY USE.

Purity
and
Excellence
of
Materials
in
Manufacture

TRADE
MARK

THE
B&E
B.C?

Purity
and
Excellence
of
Materials
in
Manufacture

THE TANNHAEUSER BEER is brewed from the Finest Pale Canada
West Barley Malt and Saazer Hops, and especially recommended for
its tonic and nutritive qualities. It is richly packed in attractive
glass bottles for Family Use. BERGNER & ENGEL received TWO
MEDALS at the Centennial Exhibition and were awarded the GRAND
PRIZE at the Universal Exposition in Paris, 1878.

The Bergner & Engel Brewing Co

PHILADELPHIA.

A. VON N. ROSENEGK, Manager,
Hancock and Marshall streets, Richmond, VA.

ly 5

Alfred von Nickisch Rosenegk made his first mark on Richmond in the
1880s as manager of the local branch of Bergner & Engel Brewing
Company. *Library of Congress, Chronicling America.*

One source said Rosenegk actually arrived in Richmond in 1882, but accounts agree that by 1885 he had replaced Theodor Bartz as manager of Bergner & Engel's Richmond operation. He watched as more "come-here" breweries flocked to the city on the James: Gerke and Christian Moerlein, both from Cincinnati; Joseph Schlitz from you know where; Crescent from who knows where; Louis Bergdoll from Philadelphia; George Ehret and his Hell Gate Lager from New York; and Darley Park from Baltimore. The Maryland brewery settled in on the corner of Adams and Canal Streets and ran a full-page ad in the 1891 city directory touting its "Extra Fine Pale and Standard Lager Beers."

There was another development to keep an eye on, this in the political sphere. The Virginia General Assembly passed a bill in 1886 giving localities the option of holding special elections to determine if liquor licenses should be granted. The measure, according to a front-page article in the *Richmond Dispatch*, "brings the people of Virginia face to face with one of the greatest issues presented in recent years…Soon there will be two great parties in the state: one wet; the other, dry."

The forces of temperance were on the move, and as we shall see in the new century, their strength was not to be underestimated. Both Rosenegk and Stumpf predicted Richmond would not become a "dry" town. Indeed, on Monday, April 26, 1886, residents in Richmond voted to be "wet" by a resounding margin of 5,681 votes out of 8,941 total. Manchester, then a city, also voted "very wet."

Though passions and rhetoric sometimes became inflamed, "Richmond has the right to congratulate herself upon the good sense and good temper displayed by her people from the beginning to the ending of the contest," wrote the *Richmond Dispatch*. "Few campaigns here were ever conducted more fairly, or will leave less rancor. Most of the dry people took defeat manfully, simply saying: that they hoped for better luck next time."

That day would come, but political and economic forces followed a different wind now. Beer—hometown beer—was about to flow in unprecedented fashion in the River City.

4

THE TITANS OF PRE-PROHIBITION

The morning weather was not promising. Clouds hovered, allowing the October sun only brief peeks through the canopy. Light showers fell intermittently, and a soggy chill threatened to dampen the mood.

Richmond's German community, however, was not to be dispirited. "It is safe to say that had it rained in torrents, German ardor would not have been restrained. The German heart was in the celebration," reported the *Richmond Dispatch*.

Indeed, German Day on Monday, October 6, 1890, was a celebration of undeniable vigor. Thousands thronged to cheer a parade of young men, to listen and dance to the bands and orchestra, to observe Volkfest demonstrations at the Exposition Grounds, to hear speeches and, yes, to drink beer. The all-day event was of such significance that the *Dispatch* devoted its entire eight-column front page to coverage, including four columns for the keynote address *in German*—"printed so that all natives may read it with pride."

Such was the stature and influence of the German community as the decade began. And one of the chief figures was Alfred von Nickisch Rosenegk, grand chief marshal of the morning procession and the welcoming speaker. "Germany is our mother; the United States of America is the bride of our choice…But in this great and wonderful Union there is a third, our Virginia, our beautiful Virginia, in which we found our beloved home, Richmond."

Hometown pride spurred a remarkable moment in Richmond's beer history. Rosenegk and Peter Stumpf, also an influential member of the

Alfred von Nickisch Rosenegk rose to prominence in the German community and founded his brewery in 1891. *Virginia Historical Society.*

community, had seen the success of the "come-here" breweries—including Anheuser-Busch, which Stumpf represented, and Bergner & Engel, which was Rosenegk's charge. The two men decided the time was right to take things local. Their ambitions were to collide, however, in almost comic fashion.

Rosenegk partnered with Emil Kersten, formerly head brewer at a Charleston, South Carolina brewery. On June 3, 1891, the *Dispatch* reported that their brewery was under construction near the Exposition Grounds. In late August, the birth of Richmond Brewery was celebrated with a parade, "and it is understood that the product will be put upon the market today."

The facility, located on Hermitage Road next to the crossing of the Richmond, Fredericksburg and Potomac (RF&P) Railroad (where the Todd Lofts building is today), boasted two imposing four-story buildings—one a brew house and the other for storage. Inside were two copper steam kettles of one hundred and two hundred barrels' capacity, a twenty-four-ton ice machine and two boilers.

Before the year was out, Richmond Brewery was bottling Standard, Pale Extra, Dark Extra and Famous Export beers. The final line of one newspaper ad had this pitch: "Give home industry a fair show by trying it in the original packages."

While Rosenegk was trumpeting Richmond Brewery, Stumpf was launching Richmond Brewing Company. Confusing? To say the least. Just months after opening in July 1892, Richmond Brewing Company was renamed Peter Stumpf Brewing Company.

Above: Peter Stumpf (left center, leaning on the sign) and employees at his brewery posed for a photo in the early days of the business. *Courtesy of Chip Stumpf family.*

Right: Stressing the healthful aspects of beer was a prime marketing tool of Home Brewing Company, as shown in this 1912 ad in the *Richmond Times-Dispatch. Library of Congress, Chronicling America.*

Its site, at the corner of Harrison and Clay Streets, might ring a bell. It was the home of Edward Euker's brewery, taken over by George Robinson and his Eagle Brewery after the Yuengling venture at Rocketts Landing closed. And speaking of eagles—Stumpf's trademark showed our venerable national bird with wings raised, perched on a stump and holding in its beak ropes attached to a small keg bearing the initials "PS." Remember that Stumpf had been an agent for Anheuser-Busch, which sported an eagle emblem. And Yuengling not only started in Pottsville, Pennsylvania, as the Eagle Brewery but also used baldie for its logo. Eagles certainly were not an endangered species in Richmond beer circles.

Stumpf's brewery also had an impressive layout, with a brew house, malt house, bottling department, office building, stables, cooperage, refrigeration apparatus and storage departments covering a block and a half. The total value of buildings and equipment was $150,000. A garden and summer resort adjoined the brewery, which was less than a mile from Rosenegk's.

Wrangling Over a Blue Ribbon

The business included Stumpf's brother, Joseph, as secretary-treasurer, and Ernest Meyer, formerly of Philadelphia, as brewmaster. Two other prominent Richmond businessmen, John D. Doyle and George Guvernator, were on the board. "These gentlemen were induced to venture upon this enterprise by reason of the demand for beer of home manufacture," an 1892 newspaper ad says. Indeed, the leading brand was "Home Beer," and the ad prominently trumpets the new "Home Brewery." This presages a name change in 1897 to Home Brewing Company.

As if things weren't tangled enough between these two, an incident at the 1892 State Exposition, the equivalent of today's State Fair of Virginia, put some thorns in the thicket. Judges awarded "premiums," aka ribbons, for everything from cattle to cantaloupe—and for lager beer. Rosenegk's Richmond Brewery initially won the top prize. What ensued is best described in a colorful *Richmond Dispatch* account that ran on October 16, 1892, under the heading "Wrangle About a Premium":

> *Protest against this decision was made by the Peter Stumpf Brewing Company, and a new committee of five was appointed to "sit on" the*

Home Brewing Company's exhibit at the State Fair of Virginia emphasized the medicinal and healthful properties of beer, a common claim in the years before Prohibition. *Virginia Historical Society.*

question. The samples from the two breweries were served so that the judges could not tell which was which. Several "big, large schooners" of the foaming beverage were duly disposed of, and the beer was all so good that the judges could not for the life of them decide which was better. Two favored the Richmond Brewery and two Peter Stumpf. The odd man disposed of a schooner or two, and finally it was deemed best to draw straws—not the straws through which they sucked the lager—and Peter Stumpf was an easy winner. The premium was accordingly demanded from the Richmond Brewery, and Mr. Rosenegk declared that nothing less than brute force could take away the pretty blue ribbon; and so [the superintendent] *reported the situation to headquarters.*

The coveted premium was finally obtained from Mr. Rosenegk, and was soon gracing the stand of Peter Stumpf, where lager flowed freely for some hours in honor of the event. But the grand beer festival was as brief as it was sparkling. Mr. Rosenegk at once sued out an injunction against the society, and the Chancery Court took possession of the beautiful ribbon, which at present adorns the wall of the secretary's office.

I can't read this without picturing those judges with their "big, large schooners" getting sloshed, saying, "Just one more," as they tried to decide. (Apparently, they didn't draw straws; the newspaper ran a letter the next day correcting the account, saying the premium was decided by ballot.)

The case went to court in February 1893, and needing neither schooners nor straws, the judge decided in favor of Richmond Brewery. Rosenegk and Kersten celebrated the decree with a parade that included "a large float with an immense cask, upon which was seated Gambrinus, the symbolic protector and promoter of the brewing industry."

A little thumbing of the nose? There are other indications of competitive rivalry. An 1899 Rosenegk Brewing Company ad with a sketch of a bottle asks patrons to make sure the proper label and trademark are on each bottle of its beer "as we understand our package is being very closely imitated." Just inches to the left, a Home Brewing Company ad also has a sketch of its bottle, identical in size and shape.

Variety of Styles Spans Broad Spectrum

Richmonders must have been thirsty enough to support both breweries, not only in volume but in diversity as well. Rosenegk offered Challenge, Edelbrau, Tidal Wave and Palest Export brands, plus a porter and other styles. Average alcohol content was 5 to 7 percent by volume. Home Brewing Company also sold several brands, including Weiner, XXX Brown Stout, Extra-Brew Porter, Piedmont Export, Standard Lager and the flagship Richbrau lager. At one point, the brewery offered twenty-five dollars in gold to the person who suggested the best name for a new beer. The winner—Hombruco! (Get it? Home Brew Company.)

Local drinkers had additional options in the 1890s and 1900s from "come-here" breweries, though some ventures lasted only briefly. At various times, you could order Ballantine's Export Beer. Or Bergner & Engel's Tannhaeuser, "unquestionably the finest light beer extant." Or "Fine as Silk" Dixie Beer from Old Dominion Brewing Company. Maybe some "sparking with life" Perfect Brew from Monumental Brewing

Monumental Brewing Company was not alone in claiming to sell the world's best bottled beer. *Cook Collection, Valentine Richmond History Center.*

Company? Some Tivoli or Vienna Cabinet from Portner? Pilsner Cabinet Lager Beer ("It Is Absolutely Pure") from Gerke of Cincinnati? Perhaps Pabst ("No family should be without it")? Schlitz? Before it was making Milwaukee famous, it was billing itself in big, bold letters in the *Richmond Dispatch* as "The Beer That Makes No Man Bilious."

Anheuser-Busch evolved during this period as well. An 1899 ad in the *Richmond Times* trumpets a new brew—Black & Tan, "the American Porter"—joining its stable of Original Budweiser, Faust, Michelob, Anheuser Standard, Pale Lager and Anheuser-Busch Dark. A few years later, the St. Louis giant was celebrating its growth from 8,000 barrels nationwide in 1865 to 1,109,315 barrels in 1902, making it the largest brewery in the world.

A familiar name, Joseph Stumpf, headed A-B's management in Richmond during this period. He had been secretary-treasurer of the Peter Stumpf Brewing Company, but he resigned after a salary dispute in 1894. The next year saw him at A-B, and "to his brother and the other breweries that came

This ad makes it clear that Mrs. Henry Bucker had taken the reins in her deceased husband's business. *1891 Richmond City Directory.*

to Richmond, Joseph Stumpf provided stiff competition for the next 21 years," writes Danny Morris.

Other changes were afoot. Peter Stumpf stepped down in 1897 as president and focused his energy on a café downtown and on the Merchants Cold Storage and Ice Company. Perhaps because of the strain of various business interests, his health deteriorated, and in 1903, he died at his home on East Marshall Street. The brewery, however, flourished. On April 1, 1897, the name had been changed to Home Brewing Company, and Fritz Sitterding, who succeeded Stumpf as president, led the business into new markets in Virginia and North Carolina. Fresh energy also came in 1898 from brewmaster George N. Bernier, a graduate of the American Brewing Academy in Chicago. (Take note of these names, Bernier and Sitterding, for their stamp on HBC continued for generations.)

One local enterprise that took an opposite direction was that of Henry Bucker and his wife, Elizabeth. From the early 1880s, Bucker had operated a saloon and "steam bottling" business on East Main Street. Their personal life suffered a blow in 1885, when their only daughter, Mary Pauline, died at the age of one year, three months. Four years later, Henry died, leaving the bottling operation to Elizabeth.

Oddly, newspaper ads continued to promote the business as Henry Bucker's, while those in city directories of the time made it clear that Mrs. Bucker was at the helm. Regardless, by 1891, the Bucker name was tied to the Joseph Schlitz and George Ehret breweries. That summer, Cincinnati's Christian Moerlein Brewing Company announced in a bold ad that Bucker had become the agent for its "celebrated beers." The *Richmond Dispatch* wrote glowingly of this development, as Moerlein's beer was "all the rage…Heretofore we have never had such a beverage. It has caught on like wild-fire."

Something happened. Details are elusive, but by the end of the decade, the operation had fizzled. A business listing in 1898 includes Mrs. Henry Bucker as operating a brewery, but in January 1900, the Christian Moerlein Company went to court seeking $854.05 in unpaid accounts from her. Less than two weeks later, Elizabeth Bucker declared bankruptcy in U.S. District Court.

BUSINESSES FAIL AFTER FINANCIAL PANIC

One potential cause might have been the Panic of 1893. It was far more severe than the financial crisis two decades earlier, leading to the failure of more than five hundred banks and fifteen thousand businesses across the country. Recovery didn't start until 1897, and a newspaper snapshot of manufacturers that year shows our two locals surviving, along with Anheuser-Busch, Portner and Bergner & Engel.

Kersten and Rosenegk, however, weren't doing so well; 1897 marked the dissolution of their partnership. The business had been operating as Richmond Brewery and Hygeia Ice Factory (more about the ice business in a minute), but the two entities were split, and Kersten was bought out for $105,000. He still held a deed of trust to the building, though, and when Rosenegk started making changes to the facility, Kersten sought—and was granted—an injunction against further alterations.

Let's leave that court battle to look at something that we of the air-conditioned refrigeration age might find difficult to appreciate: ice! Ice as big business. Ice as a daily necessity. Both local breweries included ice factories, the Hygeia as mentioned and the Consumers Ice Company of Sitterding's outfit. A situation in 1911 illuminates the intensity of need among the

Before refrigeration, businesses like the Consumers Ice Company were important to sustain Home Brewing Company's operation. *Valentine Richmond History Center.*

populace. During a withering heat wave in July that year (we all know about Richmond summers), the supply of ice in town hit a nadir. The situation became dire one weekend when blue laws prohibited sales on Sunday. What to do? Send for the cavalry!

> *Summoned from church by an almost panic-stricken employee, Fritz Sitterding hurried yesterday to the plant of the Consumers Ice Company, Harrison and Clay streets, of which he is president, and found a crowd of more than 500 men, women, and children clamoring for ice. Mr. Sitterding lost no time in ordering the place thrown open to supply the public with what it wanted—ice. Despite the Sunday laws, he felt no hesitancy in meeting the demands of the sweltering people.*

Tending to the health of the populace did not always take such dramatic action for our brewers. In fact, beer more than ice was touted for its health value. "It supplies nearly all the liquid and solid nourishment necessary to sustain life. It furnishes nutriment in the most highly assimilable form," declares a 1910 Home Brewing Company ad.

Rosenegk declared in a 1912 ad: "Purity and healthfulness are combined in our Challenge and Edelbrau brands of bottled beer…The purest materials, with an absolute cleanliness results in a temperance drink of unsurpassed delight." (Note the word "temperance.")

A Schlitz ad read: "Your home will be healthier when you keep bottled Schlitz. The barley is food—the hops are a tonic. And the drinking of liquids flushes the system of waste." And lest we forget about the bilious factor: "Be sure that the beer is aged, so it will not cause biliousness."

The industry's efforts to educate people on the positives of beer went beyond nutrition. Home Brewing Company in particular put on intriguing exhibits at the State Fair of Virginia. In 1912, a miniature brew house, complete with tanks and a bottling line, was built, and a New York expert was brought in to lecture on the process. In 1913, an exhibit with "an ever-flowing bottle of beer in the centre of a lunch table" drew a stream of attendees.

One sentence in that *Richmond Times-Dispatch* account takes note of a growing conflict: "There are many people visiting the fair who do not approve of the business of the Home Brewing Company or any company engaged in that kind of business, but all the same everybody, including the preachers and the temperance orators, stop at the Home Brewing Company's booth to study and even admire the novel display it has there."

FORCES OF TEMPERANCE SURGE

Yes, the forces of temperance had not only resurfaced but were also gaining strength. Another current further roiled the tide of the times—strong loyalty in the German American community for the Motherland and pride in its military might as World War I loomed.

The themes played out in extraordinary fashion. "Prohibition menaced not only the brewers and the men on their payrolls, the large number of saloon and beer-garden owners and liquor dealers; it would also deprive the German clubs of their major source of income, the profits from beer sales at their get-togethers…What German could conceive of meeting over soft drinks?" wrote Klaus Wust in *The Virginia Germans*.

Brewers had deep pockets, and Rosenegk, Sitterding and others mustered opposition to Prohibition. The "wet" and "dry" forces seemed headed for a showdown in the late summer of 1914. The outbreak of war in Europe, however, cast a different light on German Americans, already disparaged in some circles for their beer-loving ways. "While most Richmonders stared in disbelief, the Germans in their midst reenacted the jubilant scenes of the Kaiser's mobilization," Wust wrote. America was officially neutral, but the undisguised zeal displayed by many German Americans did not sit well with much of the larger community. Prejudice and persecution grew.

That year, 1914, also was a turning point in the politics of Virginia's prohibition battle. Twice before, legislators had proposed unsuccessfully holding a statewide referendum on staying wet or going dry. Efforts by the Anti-Saloon League and its Virginia leader, Reverend James Cannon Jr.—plus some maneuvering within political circles of the time—yielded results in 1914. The referendum was set for September; in the months leading to the vote, bitter words flew. Temperance advocates attacked alcohol as a poison (one reason so many beer ads emphasized nutritional value) and alcoholic beverages as feeding immoral behavior. Opponents said prohibition would violate the principle of local self-government, reduce revenues and increase crime because people would drink anyway.

The choice was simple. Voters picked either "For State-Wide Prohibition" or "Against State-Wide Prohibition." The measure for prohibition passed by a count of 94,251 to 63,886. Richmond and three other cities—Arlington, Norfolk and Williamsburg—voted wet. Legislators quickly approved a new law, called the Mapp Act after state senator Walter Mapp. It declared that as of November 1, 1916, Virginia would be dry. Specifically, the Mapp Act made it illegal to, among other things, manufacture, transport, sell or keep for sale ardent spirits. Porter, ale, beer and all malt liquors were included. You were allowed to keep a certain amount—"one quart of whisky, or one gallon of wine, or three gallons of beer within a period of thirty days"—for strictly personal use. Breweries and distilleries could operate if they sold their products out of state.

An effort was made in mid-1916 to allow breweries to use an unorthodox process to continue operating. It involved breaking beer down into two products, a soft drink containing no alcohol and pure commercial alcohol. The hope was that "expensive brewery plants in Richmond, Norfolk, Alexandria, Roanoke, and other points in the State, now doomed under the prohibition law, may be spared annihilation and even made more profitable than ever," the *Times-Dispatch* reported. The idea became moot when the Mapp Act was interpreted to prohibit the sale of any malt beverages, intoxicating or not. That also ruled out near beer, another potential avenue to survival.

As the countdown to Virginia's prohibition reached its final days, newspapers chronicled the scene. "Urgent preparedness appeals have been conspicuous in every saloon. The man who takes his daily eye-opener and his nightly sleep-producer has been warned of the dry times ahead. Many dealers have completed arrangements for removing their business to other territory. Still others are ready to embark upon untried business ventures," reported the *Times-Dispatch*.

When the actual moment came at midnight on October 31, church bells chimed, Halloween revelers partied and prohibitionists rallied to pray and give thanks. Saloon patrons downed their last public drink, although thousands of gallons had been stored in private homes. "In Richmond alone, dealers estimate that $2,000,000 had been spent in stocking cellars," the *News Leader* reported.

The night passed peacefully in Richmond. Only a handful of people were arrested for drunkenness. The *Times-Dispatch* noted that Virginia became the eighteenth state to ban intoxicating beverages, constituting a dry swath across the South.

In two years, the rest of the nation would follow. In Richmond, seventeen years would pass before beer would flow from local taps.

5
KRUEGER MAKES HISTORY,
RICHBRAU BECOMES HISTORY

The aftermath of Halloween 1916 presented a frightening future for businesses that had anything to do with alcohol. Many localities in the state had already exercised their option to go dry. Still, approximately eight hundred saloons closed their doors as prohibition became Virginia law. Richmond's toll, according to the *Times-Dispatch* of November 1, 1916, was as follows: "One hundred and forty-one retail dealers, seventeen retailers and shippers, six wholesalers, ten social clubs, four rectifiers, and two manufacturers of malt liquors."

Among the state's six breweries, Portner closed immediately. Others continued until nationwide Prohibition came in 1918. Sadly, the Rosenegk Brewing Company was one of the early victims, and the impact took a personal toll on its founder. "Rosenegk family members have said that when Alfred von N. Rosenegk's love of brewing was halted by prohibition, he became ill," writes beer historian Danny Morris. Indeed, the obituary after Rosenegk's death in August 1917 at the family's summer home in Virginia Beach read, "His business interests in Richmond were extensive, but it is said that perhaps his greatest interest commercially was in the brewery established by him in Richmond."

Survival meant change. For some, that meant new products. Consider Alpha, "the drink sensation of the age." Newspaper ads carried testimony from scientists who "reported they could find nothing to identify it as a malt beverage...[It is] a drink that 'hits the spot' without intoxicating or producing other harmful effects produced by alcoholic liquors."

This 1916 ad for Bevo not only meets the non-intoxicating criterion of the day but also offers food-pairing suggestions. *Library of Congress, Chronicling America.*

Pabst and Anheuser-Busch also introduced temperance drinks—the former with Pablo, the latter with Bevo. A 1916 *Times-Dispatch* ad for Bevo describes it as "a cereal beverage, not a near beer." Would that cereal perhaps be malt? In one of the oddest food-pairing suggestions of the millennium,

A-B touted, "You cannot enjoy Dutch lunches, Welsh rarebits, oysters, clams, lobsters, sausage, cheese, and many other such delicious edibles without partaking of a little Bevo." (How about a burger and fries?)

For Home Brewing Company, survival meant a temporary vanishing act. In October 1916, ads announced it would cease to exist, being succeeded by the Buchanan Spring Company, still at the corner of Harrison and Clay. One of the products was "Dix Brannew," a nonmalt, nonalcoholic drink in the mold of Bevo, Parvo and Alpha: "Its rich amber color, its creamy white form and its lively sparkle delight the eye."

Where beer once was brewed, water and soda took the limelight. Sitterding and his colleagues arranged to lease bottling facilities at Harrison and Clay to the Beaufont Company, renowned for its soft drinks—the ginger ale was "as invigorating as a breeze from the North Pole, as healthful as a draught from the Fountain of Youth." Beaufont's name, and its bottled water, came from Beaufont Spring in Chesterfield County (near where the Boulders office complex is today).

Another source of income was ice. Three ice plants, including that operated by the Buchanan Spring Company, merged into a single entity, Richmond Ice Delivery Corporation, with Sitterding at the helm. As home refrigerators grew more common, however, the business lost its edge, and it was sold in 1927.

The end of a different era would come the following year with the death of Fritz Sitterding. Like Stumpf and Rosenegk, he had come to the United States from Germany, a nineteen-year-old former soldier weary of war and eager for opportunity. He spoke no English and could barely rub two nickels together, but he learned the construction trade and helped start a lumber business. He got into brewing in the days of beer gardens and band concerts in the parks, and the affable aspects of beer played out in his personality. He was a man of "alert wit and humor and [had] the friendliness of a man who spoke to everybody," recalled a *Times-Dispatch* retrospective. Sitterding helped secure the franchise for the first company to operate an electric streetcar system, plus he had extensive interests in banking and philanthropy. He became ill early in 1928 and died on April 4 at Monroe Terrace Apartments.

The Sitterding business reins fell to Fritz Jr., and circumstances could hardly have been more challenging as the decade careened and crashed. The collapse of the stock market, among other things, triggered the Great Depression, and jobs became as scarce as good beer. "From 1929 to 1932, 100,000 businesses entered bankruptcy and more than four thousand banks shut their doors. By late 1932, 11 million adults had lost their jobs," wrote historian Maureen Ogle.

On the upside, though, the fervor for Prohibition began to cool. In his bid for the presidency, Franklin D. Roosevelt adopted repeal of the Eighteenth Amendment as a campaign platform, and after he took office in 1933, Congress acted quickly to create and send the Twenty-first Amendment on its way through state legislatures. By the end of the year, national Prohibition was history. Even before then, beer was being sold, first in 3.2 percent "near beer" and then at full strength.

Virginia was not in the first wave of states that legalized beer. But the handwriting was on the saloon wall, and folks in Richmond's brewing community lost no time preparing for the inevitable. Like a phoenix rising from the ashes of the temperance movement, Home Brewing Company was reborn in 1933 through the reorganization of two companies: Beaufont and Home Products. While the General Assembly twisted Governor John Garland Pollard's arm for a special session to legalize beer, Home Brewing Company announced plans to remodel its plant. About $275,000 would be spent on improvements, including $150,000 on new machinery, with the goal of cranking out thirty thousand barrels annually. Sitterding Jr. would continue as president, and George Bernier Sr., who had helped guide Home Products in manufacturing soft drinks, would assume the role of brewmaster. Thirty new employees would join Home Brewing, bringing the total to fifty workers. Jobs!

Just as the post-Prohibition era was poised to begin, folks raised a toast to the good old days, before evil and alcohol became synonymous. An article in the October 4, 1933 edition of the *Times-Dispatch* drew a vivid picture of Richmond's sudsy past:

> *The most popular section for saloons was the business district of Main Street, between Eighth and Fifteenth. There were two or three to every block, and they overflowed into the side streets and north to Bank and south to Cary. Here was Frank Anthony's Commercial, at 912 East Main; Stumpf's at Eighth, where Pat Quinn and Charley Raabe did the mixing, and Chris, the genial, smiling "mayor of Jackson Ward," served as head waiter and general factotum and knew all the regulars by name and remembered unfailingly their preferences.*

Also on October 4, the newspaper reported returns of the statewide referendum on repeal. To no one's surprise, Virginia voted two to one to go wet, and the following June, in the midst of a twelve-day heat wave, local beer again became a reality. Home Brewing Company delivered lager to retailers in kegs (the new bottling equipment had not arrived). In place of Hombruco, the beer of the day was Richbrau; the name stood for Richmond and the German word for "brew." You could buy bottles in two strengths: 3.2 percent or full pre-Prohibition potency.

While this chapter of history was being made, another was taking shape. In one of those weird twists of fate, another Home Brewing Company, in Newark, New Jersey, would have a link to Richmond's future. This brewery's facilities at one point were retained by Gottfried Krueger Brewing Company, also of Newark. Gottfried Krueger had deep German roots, which served him well in building a fortune in brewing, but he became a victim of anti-German sentiment. In 1918, his estate, valued at $40 million, was seized.

Krueger died in 1926, and his son William became the new president. Krueger Brewing Company had weathered Prohibition by producing near beer, so its facility was ready to run on all cylinders when repeal became reality. That led American Can officials to Krueger's door with a novel idea—putting beer in cans. What seems so common to us today was unknown in 1933, and Krueger executives were understandably reluctant. Contact with metal generally caused beer to go bad. But American Can had thought of that; it proposed a can with an enamel lining similar to that used in kegs. In addition, the can would be strong enough to withstand the pressure of carbonation and the process of pasteurization.

Let's start with a test, Krueger officials said. About two thousand cans of near beer went out to friends and faithful customers, who filled out questionnaires. Responses were enthusiastic—91 percent liked it, and 85 percent said it tasted more like draft than bottled beer. Krueger still balked, so American Can representatives sweetened the deal. They would install all of the canning equipment for free; if the idea tanked, they'd remove the equipment, also for free.

One more hedge. Instead of releasing Krueger beer in cans in their prime market, brewery officials decided on another test, in a distant market like, say, Richmond, Virginia. "It was far enough away that if cans were unpopular it wouldn't hurt Krueger's core market," says the RustyCans website.

On January 24, 1935, cans of Krueger's Cream Ale and Krueger's Finest Beer went on sale in Richmond. A large ad in the *Times-Dispatch* accompanied the release to explain this newfangled phenomenon. "Krueger's now presents the Keglined Can for Ale and Beer," the ad announced. It played up cans' advantages (smaller, lighter, shielding the beer from light) and bottles'

FOR YOUR GREATER CONVENIENCE AND ENJOYMENT

KRUEGER'S *now presents the*

KEGLINED* CAN

(Holds 12 ounces — the same as a bottle)

for ALE *and* BEER

LEFT—*Wood and metal beer kegs are COMPLETELY LINED INSIDE to protect flavor. So is our Keglined Can.*

RIGHT—*Now your Ale and Beer are FULLY PROTECTED FROM LIGHT—the enemy of flavor. Beer and Ale exposed to light gradually lose flavor.*

LEFT—*Your personal container. NO DEPOSIT TO MAKE—NO BOTTLES TO RETURN. You simply throw away the empty can.*

RIGHT—*Holds just as much as a bottle—yet TAKES ONLY HALF THE SPACE. Here's convenience you'll like—in your kitchen—in your ice-box.*

Here's the biggest news since repeal—it's the news of a modern way—a more convenient way—to enjoy Krueger's Cream Ale (formerly Boar's Head) in your home. Krueger's, always in the vanguard of brewing science, is the *first* to offer you the advantages of the new keglined can . . . advantages that are truly amazing.

Imagine buying Ale or Beer for your home without paying a bottle deposit, without the trouble and effort of making bottle returns! Imagine being able to get twice as much in the same space in your ice-box! These are the modern conveniences made possible by the astounding keglined can. Of course, you can get your Krueger's in bottles as usual, but we urge you to be one of the first to enjoy the benefits of this remarkable

REG. U.S. PAT. OFF.

keglined can development. Get a can of Krueger's Cream Ale or Krueger's Finest Beer today! G. Krueger Brewing Company, Newark, N. J.

Richmond Distributor:
CAVALIER DISTRIBUTING CORP. • RICHMOND, VA. ⚡ TEL. 4-8177

Be sure to ask your dealer for a "Quick & Easy" opener and learn the simple little trick of opening your can of ale or beer.

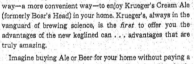

KRUEGER'S CREAM ALE

AND KRUEGER'S *Finest* BEER

also in bottles and on draught

The 1935 debut of beer in cans by Krueger Brewing Company made history in Richmond. *Richmond Times-Dispatch.*

drawbacks (having to pay deposits and make returns). It explained how to use the "quick & easy opener" (aka church key). It illustrated how linings were already used in kegs. It urged consumers to "get a can today!"

Any reservations harbored by the Krueger folks vanished quickly. The test was "a flying success." People loved canned beer. Distributors wanted it. Pabst jumped into canning with both feet. By the end of 1935, thirty-six brewers were putting beer in cans. And Richmond had put yet another chapter in its book of history.

The impetus of that success led Krueger Brewing Company to enjoy some good years, including a 100th anniversary celebration in 1958. However, "the celebration couldn't hide the fact that Krueger's was suffering a loss of market share to the national companies like Schlitz and Anheuser-Busch," says RustyCans. The company soon cashed in its chips—the Newark plant was closed, and production of the brand moved to Rhode Island.

Those same pressures came to bear on Home Brewing Company in Richmond. Competition with out-of-town breweries came quickly after Prohibition's repeal. It wasn't just the brewing giants. In 1936, Fidelio Brewery of New York touted having Richmond's bestselling beer in a newspaper ad. Globe Brewing Company of Baltimore made incursions with offerings such as Arrow 200th anniversary beer.

Home Brewing still was producing soft drinks—Tru-Ade and Climax, primarily—

ES IST SUFFIG!
--YOU'RE TELLING ME!

THE GREEKS have a word for it. So do the Germans. I don't know what the Greeks call it, but the German word for this elusive quality of RICHBRAU beer is "suffigkeit"

Briefly, it means that one bottle of RICH-BRAU makes you want another. It describes the can't-get-enough flavor of RICHBRAU. If you have tried RICH-BRAU you will naturally say, "you're telling me! If you haven't tried it, why not try it today. (Wouldn't a cold glass of RICHBRAU taste good right now?

RICHBRAU is so good because it is made of the very best of natural materials. There are no exclusive processes or secret formulaes; nothing is added or filtered out to change its natural flavor. That's why it's wise to call for RICHBRAU by name.

RICHBRAU
MADE RIGHT HERE IN RICHMOND
THE MIRTH PARADE
A riotous comedy with a great galaxy of vaudeville and radio stars, in a fast moving mirthquake of mirth, melody and music. Over WRVA every Thursday evening at 9 P. M.

Clever, eye-catching advertising, as in this 1934 ad, was a hallmark of Home Brewing Company's presence in Richmond after Prohibition. *Richmond Times-Dispatch.*

until 1960, when a newly formed business bought the machinery, formulas and patents. That freed up space for new machinery and expanded beer production, brewery officials said. Capacity eventually increased to 100,000 barrels, and Richbrau was being distributed throughout much of Virginia.

That was still small potatoes, comparatively, and by the end of the decade, operating losses made continuing unsustainable. Home Brewing Company ceased operations in December 1969. Frederick Sitterding III, president, explained in a letter to stockholders:

> *More and more companies manufacturing and marketing nationally known name brands have become interested in the Richmond and Virginia markets with the result that although the cost of materials and supplies has increased, the selling price of beer in which our company markets its products has decreased.*

A *Richmond News Leader* article added details to the nationwide trend. "According to industry sources, the number of U.S. breweries has declined from 440 to less than 90 since 1949. The top 10 brewers have 68 percent of the market." A Maryland company, Queen City Brewing Company, took over production of Richbrau.

The loss was profound. Breweries had operated at Harrison and Clay Streets since before the Civil War. Richbrau made there had quenched local thirsts for fifty years. The Sitterdings and Berniers had been company leaders for three generations. The company's beers—from the first lagers to the flagship Richbrau—had become staples among Richmond drinkers.

You can still see the "Home Brewing Company" lettering on the building at 1201 West Clay Street. If you poke inside the lobby, you'll see an antiquated grain mill. You can find old Richbrau cans, bottles and other memorabilia in the troves of collectors.

There are treasured memories as well. To be honest, the beer did not enjoy the best reputation for quality. "The original Richbrau wasn't a good beer," a professional brewer said. One old-timer was a little harsher, claiming the flavor came close to tasting like foot wash. Still, it was a hometown brewery with a strong local following.

"I was born in a keg of Richbrau. They cracked it open and I was there," said Leon Stepanian Jr. in a 1998 interview. Stepanian's father, Leon Sr., cut his teeth selling Richbrau beer, and his family, like Home Brewing Company's Sitterdings and Berniers, continues today a three-generation

Gone but not forgotten—Home Brewing Company's building at 1201 West Clay Street still brings back memories. *Photo by Lee Graves.*

tradition in the beer business at Loveland Distributing Company, where Mark Stepanian carries the torch as president.

One more footnote to history. In a 1996 interview, Leon Stepanian Sr. recalled that it could have been Home Brewing Company, not Krueger, to launch the world's first canned beer. "American Can Company was operating on Venable Street. There was a man there named Buck Fairlamb, a friend of [Fritz Sitterding Jr.]. He told Mr. Sitterding, 'American Can Company perfected a keg-lined can. We want Richbrau to be the first beer in the world to be sold in cans,'" Stepanian said.

Sitterding's response? "Beer don't belong in cans!"

6

MICROBREWING'S FIRST WAVE SURGES INTO CITY

L et's crunch some numbers. Breweries in existence in the United States when Stumpf and Rosenegk were gearing up operations in the early 1890s: more than 2,000. Breweries in existence when Home Brewing Company went out of business in 1969: just over 80. Breweries in existence in mid-2014: 3,040, and nearly 99 percent were craft breweries.

So how did the industry sink to that twentieth-century cellar and then rebound to make the United States the most prolific, creative and exciting brewing nation in the world? And how has this renaissance played out in Richmond, four centuries after John Smith and Christopher Newport first shared English beer with Native Americans?

We begin by looking at the combined forces of Prohibition, the Depression and World War II. The Eighteenth Amendment forced many breweries out of business; only a few remained to crank up the grain mills after 1933. Tastes also had changed after years of sugary soda. As the Depression intensified, disaster struck America's breadbasket. A long-term drought forced farm after farm to wither and die.

When war in Europe broke out, the United States provided massive shipments of grain to the Allies. Once Uncle Sam entered the conflict, rationing kicked in at home. With the nation's men fighting overseas, women dominated the domestic beer-buying market. So, with less grain to work with and lighter palates dictating demand, brewers cranked out tepid lagers. "By the time the war was over, the country had for more than thirty years resorted to light, highly carbonated beverages.

American beer tastes had undergone an incredible alteration," writes beer historian Gregg Smith.

Celebrated columnist Mike Royko summarized the flavor of Big Beer thusly: "I've tried them all…Regardless of what label or slogan you choose, it all tastes as if the secret brewing process involved running it through a horse."

The pendulum started to swing in a different direction when young adults, eager to explore distant lands in the 1960s, traveled to Europe and tasted the lagers of Germany and the ales of Britain. They tried to re-create those flavorful beers by brewing at home, though it was technically illegal because of an oversight when Prohibition was repealed. President Jimmy Carter changed that in 1979, and the seeds of a domestic brewing revolution grew. Sprouts had already taken root in California, where Fritz Maytag was reviving Anchor Steam Brewing Company and Jack McAuliffe was opening New Albion, the nation's first true microbrewery. In Virginia, a young man named Charlie Papazian was honing his homebrewing skills while a student at the University of Virginia. (We'll talk about him more in the next chapter.)

Small brewers, however, found themselves facing a system that seemed stacked against them. Before Prohibition, brewers could sell their beers directly to retailers. It was common as well for brewers to own saloons, selling only their products; price wars favored big-volume producers who could sustain minimal profit margins. After repeal, many states instituted a three-tiered structure in which brewers sold to wholesalers, who then distributed the beer to retailers. This created a different dynamic.

"The biggest brewers' command of larger and larger shares of the market enabled them to exercise an informal but lethal power over wholesalers," wrote beer historian Maureen Ogle. "A giant could pressure his distributors to truck his beer and only his beer; to drop competing brands; or to drop soft drinks, liquor, and wine. If the wholesaler refused, a brewery representative would show up at the warehouse and threaten to cancel the carrier's contract."

From the distributors' point of view, big-volume brewers offered steady income. Why make space on the truck for a local, small-potatoes brewer with no track record at the expense of a sure thing? Tastes were definitely changing, though, and imports like Heineken, Lowenbrau and Guinness benefited. During the 1960s, imports garnered less than 1 percent of the overall beer market, but the sector took off to the tune of 9 percent annual growth.

Those were the forces facing Richmond's wholesalers. Brown Distributing Company, founded in 1919, grew from a soda bottling business to a powerhouse, acquiring the Anheuser-Busch franchise in Richmond and Petersburg (as well as an area of Florida). Loveland Distributing

Company, founded in 1953 and purchased by Leon Stepanian Sr. in 1958, put its domestic focus on Miller and Coors products, with Corona leading the imports. Specialty Beverage of Virginia entered the market in 1991 with a focus on imports and microbrews. At various times, the field included other players, such as Howard, Commonwealth and J.W. Phillips distributing companies.

Virginia had become home to the giants. In 1972, Anheuser-Busch opened a brewery in Williamsburg capable of cranking out 3.2 million barrels per year of various brands (that figure grew to 8.5 million barrels in 2012). In the Shenandoah Valley, Coors built a $90 million plant in 1987 to package beers shipped from the home brewery in Golden, Colorado; the Elkton facility underwent a $300 million expansion, yielding an actual brewery in 2007 with a capacity of 7.0 million barrels annually. Miller Brewing Company, purchased by Richmond-based Philip Morris in 1969, eyed Chesterfield County as a possible location for a $220 million brewery and canning operating, but in 1975, the company decided against taking an option on the land.

CRAFT BREWING MAKES ITS DEBUT IN VIRGINIA

While the behemoths were staking out territory, a smaller enterprise was plotting a different course in Virginia Beach. In 1982, two homebrewing buddies—Jim Kollar, a veterinarian, and Lou Peron, an orthodontist—began building Chesapeake Bay Brewing Company in an industrial park in the Lynnhaven area. It was the first commercial craft brewery in the South, and the effort required $250,000, hours of hands-on labor and the help of both men's wives and Kollar's brother, Frank. Though Jim Kollar had taken a brewing course at the University of California–Davis, they decided to hire a professional. Wolfgang Roth, a young brewmaster living in Germany, moved to Virginia Beach to oversee production of Chesbay Amber, Chesbay Superior Lager and other beers.

The brewery struggled in a market ruled by mainstream light lagers, and Kollar sold it to a group of investors in 1986. The beers, however, won fans. At the 1986 Great American Beer Festival in Denver, Chesbay Doppelbock placed seventh out of 123 beers from forty-three breweries nationwide. The following year—the first that the GABF awarded medals in separate categories—the doppelbock took gold.

The Richbrau Brewing Company team in 1997 consisted of (from left) Mike Byrne, Bill Hill, Matthew Tlusty, Tom Leppert and Mark Cardwell. *Richmond Times-Dispatch.*

"[The doppelbock] was a hit with beer enthusiasts, but we were in the wrong place at the wrong time," Allen Young, an assistant brewer at the time, told a Hampton Roads magazine in 2013. "At that time, we were about the same size or bigger than Sierra Nevada out in California. If we had been on Chico Bay instead of the Chesapeake Bay, we might be telling a different story right now."

Chesbay Doppelbock and Chesapeake Bay Brewing Company's name would resurface in various bubbles in North Carolina and Virginia—including an odd link to a brewing outfit headquartered in Richmond. But that would occur only after microbrewing's tide flowed into the city.

In 1993, a century after the Rosenegk-Stumpf boom began, the first ripples of local brewing in Richmond resurfaced in a familiar location with a familiar name. Richbrau Brewing Company opened as a brewpub in Shockoe Slip, where taverns flourished in colonial times and cobblestones still rattle cars today. The business didn't take off until 1995, with new leadership by Mike Byrne, Tom Leppert and Bill Hill. Byrne and Leppert had worked at Sam Miller's Restaurant nearby, and Hill was a regular customer there. Though there was no connection with the old Home Brewing Company, the brewpub paid homage with photos, paintings and logos from the Richbrau of yesteryear.

Like many micros, Richbrau focused on quicker-fermenting ales rather than lagers. Using a fourteen-barrel system imported from California, the brewery developed a menu of eight beers. The flagships were the light-bodied Griffin Golden Ale, the more assertive Old Nick Pale Ale and the full-bodied Big Nasty Porter. Food, though, was Richbrau's primary focus—"great food, great service, and great beer," Byrne said.

The same combo fueled the launch of another Richmond institution in 1993: Commercial Taphouse & Grill. Though not a brewpub, the restaurant in the Fan District initially offered an "unheard-of eleven beers on draft," said Jim Dickerson, one of the original owners. The original list included Yuengling Black & Tan, Guinness Stout, Anchor Steam, Patowmack Ale (from a Virginia brewery), Stoudt's Double Bock and "something we called Nickel Bridge Lager."

"Big Event" at Commercial Taphouse

An event occurred in early 1994 that reverberates today. Legend Brewing Company, which had begun brewing just months before on the south side of the James River, delivered the first-ever keg of Legend Brown Ale to Commercial Taphouse. Banners were hung from the ceiling, and staff and guests were decked out for the affair.

"It was a big event. It was incredibly exciting. We were wearing ties with blue denim shirts—that's what everybody wore back then," recalls James Talley, former president and co-founder of the restaurant. "The flavor was so big for that day. It was full, rich and delicious, and this was back when you couldn't get fresh beer."

The Brown Ale was one of four recipes created by Legend owner Tom Martin with the help of his father. Brewing was in their blood. Mr. Martin worked for Anheuser-Busch as vice-president of European Brewing Operations and as the original brewmaster at the A-B Williamsburg plant. Young Martin was drawn to the profession and went to the University of California–Davis to earn a master's degree in brewing science. He put in a stint brewing for A-B in Tampa, but the efforts of pioneers like Maytag and McAuliffe prodded him to branch out on his own.

"While I was at UC-Davis, we'd go around and tour different breweries that had just started. Sierra Nevada had just started at that time," Martin said. "New Albion was around for a few years there. That was really neat because it was only a one-barrel system made out of a stainless-steel, fifty-five-gallon drum. The beer was adequate, but they had a neat pub and a beer garden."

In 1993, Martin settled on a spot on West Seventh Street in an industrial part of the old Manchester district just south of the James. It took vision to look beyond the weeds, smelly trash, scruffy trees, ugly buildings and groaning trains. "Through [everything] that was growing up, there was a very nice view of the city," Martin said in a 1998 interview. "I thought, 'This is a nice spot, right here. Right over this end a deck could be built eventually, and we could have a great location.' Of course, at the time, there was a dump right there," he said and laughed.

Brewing began in a ten-barrel system with a small tasting room; a sister company, Legendary Distributors, was established to get the beer to market (this skirted established wholesalers, an effort to gain more control of the product). In the early days, Virginia's alcohol laws required that food be served if beer was to be sold, so sandwiches were offered in a small tasting room. It wasn't much more than a one-man show, so if a client needed a keg during bar hours, Martin would have to drop everything so he or one of his few co-workers could make the delivery.

With the help of employees like brewer Alan Williamson and office manager Rob "Barley Bob" Barker, the Brown Ale, along with Legend

Pilsner, Porter and Lager, established a following and a solid foundation for the brewery. In addition, its success, along with that of Richbrau and other breweries popping up around the state, gave incentive for more local beer lovers to make the leap into commercial brewing.

JAMES RIVER, MOBJACK BAY AND OTHERS ON THE SCENE

One of those beer lovers was James Zobel, who formed James River Brewing Company in 1995 with financial help from his father, Lee. Operating in a space on Dabney Road, just outside the city limits in Henrico County, Zobel and head brewer Scott George made a mark with memorable brews like Blueberry Wheat Ale. But as with the Chesbay folks, they learned that good beers don't guarantee business success. After two years, James River folded.

Another 1995 start-up, Williamsville Brewery, fared better, though its first local venture raised eyebrows. Williamsville opened a brewery inside the Paramount Kings Dominion theme park amid whooshing roller coasters and squealing youngsters. Headed by Hanover County entrepreneur Bob Cabaniss, Williamsville had its offices in Ashland but developed breweries elsewhere—Wilmington, North Carolina; Amelia Island, Florida; and even St. Martin in the Caribbean. Cabaniss saw opportunity on Main Street in Richmond in 1999, but we'll get to that in a minute.

The Dabney Road space abandoned by James River did not remain vacant for long. Tom Swartzwelder, a former lawyer, grabbed the location and the head brewer in 1997 to birth Mobjack Bay Brewing Company. Unlike the stereotypical micro owner, Swartzwelder did not begin as a homebrewer. "I was one of those kids in the '70s that was a beer can fanatic," he said in a 1997 interview. "I had about 1,800 beer cans at the time." While growing up in Wilson, North Carolina, he would read brewing trade magazines; while visiting friends and family in Pennsylvania, he would hang out at Yuengling, Iron City and other breweries.

Swartzwelder moved from Atlanta to Virginia with his wife, Erika, who had worked with Merrill Lynch. On a previous visit, they had seen a run-down building in Gloucester and envisioned transforming it into a restaurant. They left behind the big jobs and pursued their dreams, she

Tom Swartzwelder (left) and Scott George hold a six-pack of Mobjack Bay Pale Ale, released in 1998. *Richmond Times-Dispatch.*

with the restaurant and he with Mobjack Bay. Another Gloucester resident, airline pilot Roger Anderson, was looking for an investment and pitched in as co-owner.

At the time, George was twenty-six and the youngest brewer in Richmond. To Swartzwelder, that was an advantage over someone with more professional experience. "You're never going to be unique in your own right if you just keep going out and buying recipes of these master brewers who have been doing it for years," Swartzwelder said. "To be cutting edge requires an infusion of new ideas." Those ideas led to Mobjack Bay's flagship pale ale and seasonals such as Old Coot Stout and Ballyhoo White Ale.

Another brewing entity was calling Richmond home, though in name only. Rock Creek Brewing Company, founded by entrepreneur Jon

Esposito, established headquarters here but used a Pennsylvania brewery to produce ales with local connections—Black Raven Porter (think Edgar Allan Poe), Devil's Elbow IPA (a crook in the James River) and River City ESB. Try to follow this twist of events: Rock Creek later moved production to a brewery in Raleigh, North Carolina; said facility and the Rock Creek line of beers were purchased by—wait for it—a group called Chesapeake Bay Brewing Company (it went belly up in 2003). The Chesbay Doppelbock would also be revived in Tidewater by the Virginia Brewing Company (also went belly up), and the name of the South's first craft brew would be taken by Chesbay Distributing Company in Chesapeake (acquired by Reyes Beverage Group in 2012). (Sorry for the whiplash there; deep breath.)

With so much going on, Richmond became ripe for a signature beer event. Hence, the River City Real Beer Fest. Begun modestly in the early 1990s, the festival hit a few cobblestones in the first years but found its stride by 1998. For two days, people could stroll in the historic Farmers' Market area of Shockoe Bottom and quaff forty-four beers from twenty-two breweries, all but three of which were from Virginia, Maryland or D.C.

A big jolt of the energy came from the James River Homebrewers. Members pulled taps, hosted educational seminars and, most important, tied in the annual statewide Dominion Cup homebrewing competition. A funny footnote to the 1998 event was that the Great American Beer Festival went on the road that year, and the Richmond event coincided with the weekend that the GABF was in Baltimore. Many Richmond beer lovers managed to squeeze in both events.

Speaking of the GABF, the Denver event was growing by leaps and lagers, and the prestige of winning a medal there gained cachet. Old Dominion Brewing Company in Ashburn, then the state's premier craft brewery, brought home gold, and others in northern Virginia, such as Bardo Rodeo and Sweetwater, also made Virginia proud. Richmonders, though, never found that spotlight. Richbrau gave it a concentrated shot in 1998 after brewer Favio Garcia came to Richmond from Bardo Rodeo. Festivalgoers raved about Richbrau's beers, particularly the Big Nasty Porter, but the judges picked others. "We got comments from them like 'Nice try. Wrong category,'" Byrne said.

MAIN STREET OPENING MAKES SPLASH

That doesn't mean Richmond brews lacked fans among the beer elite. Mobjack Bay Pale Ale received positive reviews in *All About Beer* magazine. Beer journalist Fred Eckhardt wrote glowingly, "Great aromatics here, good color and, best of all, there ARE hops in this fine beer." Michael Jackson, of Beer Hunter fame, praised its balance, fullness and drinkability. Jackson also included Richbrau's Tell Tale Ale, a barleywine aged in wine casks, in his *Ultimate Beer* book and spent an afternoon in 1995 sampling the wares at Legend, methodically scribbling in his reporter's notepad and posing for snapshots.

As the decade raced toward the millennium, Legend and Richbrau grew their beer lists and expanded distribution. A spacious deck and 180-seat restaurant drew beer lovers to Legend. History came full circle to Richbrau when Loveland picked up distribution of its beers (remember that Leon Stepanian Sr. sold Richbrau for Home Brewing Company in his salad years). Richbrau also developed a relationship with Old Dominion's Jerry Bailey, a Virginia craft beer pioneer, and began having beers contract-brewed at the Ashburn facility.

In 1995, legendary British beer writer Michael Jackson (right) visited Legend Brewing Company to sample the beers. Owner-founder Tom Martin (left) and Lindsay Weiford shared the moment. *Courtesy of Legend Brewing Company.*

Bob Cabaniss, president of Main Street Beer Company, launched the enterprise in 1999 in Richmond as part of the brewing portfolio that included Williamsville Brewery Limited. *Richmond Times-Dispatch.*

The biggest splash of 1999 occurred when Cabaniss opened Main Street Beer Company. The bar area appealed to the hip crowd with a stone floor, poured concrete bar and stainless-steel tables. The beers—ManGo, Work Beer, Fan Lager and others—had a target. "The goal here is to get the Budweiser and the Miller Lite drinkers to experiment," Cabaniss said. (Oh, there was another splash—Governor Jim Gilmore declared May as Virginia Beer Month to coincide with the River City Real Beer Fest.)

Meanwhile, the Florida-based chain Hops Restaurant Bar-Brewery opened a location on West Broad Street, the sixty-third store in its chain (another link in the chain later landed in the Chesterfield Towne Center complex). The backbone of the brewery's offerings included Clearwater Light, Lightning Bold Gold, Thoroughbred Red and Alligator Ale.

The new decade, however, saw setbacks to local brewing. Rumblings had already cracked the heady optimism of the movement. The failure rate of microbreweries increased in 1997 and then stabilized. "In 1995, 804

The River City Beer & Seafood Festival drew throngs to Brown's Island in 2001. *Venture Richmond.*

breweries were operating, with 287 openings and only 27 closings. Openings hit a peak at 333 in 1996, but plummeted to 183 in 1998. In those same years, closings more than tripled, from 36 in 1996 to 122 in 1998," the *Richmond Times-Dispatch* reported.

On the positive side of the scales, Richbrau went through a major expansion in 2001, adding beer equipment, a fourth bar and taps to the pool tables and dance club. Extra Billy's restaurant in Midlothian revved up a small brewery with Bill Ehlert at the paddle. Pete Slosberg of Pete's Wicked and homebrewing guru Charlie Papazian came through town to deliver their messages about flavorful beer.

On the negative side, sponsors of Richmond's signature beer festival— Downtown Presents and the Mid-Atlantic Association of Craft Brewers—split over philosophical differences in 2001, leading to a craft beer festival one weekend and a beer-and-seafood event the next. Mobjack Bay closed in 2003. Main Street Beer Company followed in 2004. Rock Creek had already gone to North Carolina.

Richbrau and Legend stood alone. Then came the financial turmoil of 2008 and the ensuing recession. Byrne, then owner, brought in a partner and steered Richbrau through renovations and a new menu, but hotel rooms were going vacant. Downtown lunch crowds were thinning. "I thought I could grab the bull by the horns and do well," Byrne said. "But all of a sudden, there just weren't the people. I walked into the worst recession since 1930."

Legend was faring better. To keep up with demand, it abandoned its sister company to go with Brown Distributing Company in 2009. The Brown Ale in particular was proving a stalwart, both in terms of customer demand and critical acclaim—it had been named a grand champion at the 2005–6 U.S. Beer Tasting Championship.

The winter of 2009–10 was not kind. Multiple snows hit on successive weekends, crippling Richbrau's business. In February, after fifteen years in the brewpub business on East Cary Street, Byrne filed for bankruptcy protection. Nearby business owners expressed shock and dismay. "It's kind of sad," said one Shockoe Slip businesswoman. "It was a Richmond staple."

It was a devastating blow for Byrne and his forty employees. "Most of the people working for me had been with me for most of those fifteen years," he said. "That was the hard part. These were career people."

Chapter 7 regulations forbade Byrne from removing anything from the building—including all of the Home Brewing Company memorabilia. But his employees wanted to salute the brewpub with one last toast. So Byrne slid two kegs out a side door, and Richbrau once again was history.

As 2010 dawned, only one brewery stood in the city of Richmond.

7
HOMEBREWERS PUT BACKBONE IN BREWING SCENE

D an Mouer was no stranger to Richmond, having come during summer vacations to visit relatives. By the time he settled here in 1973 to study at Virginia Commonwealth University, he'd been to Vietnam and Woodstock. In addition, he'd been introduced to homebrewing.

"My first job was with Westinghouse doing research in Pennsylvania. They hired me because I had a chemistry background. My boss was a chemist as well, and he and a friend made wine and beer," Mouer said. "Those guys were serious."

He was blown away by the flavor. So while studying and teaching in Richmond, he began experimenting on his own. "I was anxious to find out how to make good beer." He also was eager to connect with some kindred spirits. There weren't many around in the early 1980s, but a few places in the area sold supplies, so there must some homebrewers, he thought.

He'd purchased brewing ingredients at Bacchus and Beef, so one day late in 1982, Mouer went into the Broad Street location intending to post a notice inviting interested parties to get together. To his surprise, a fellow named Mark Stansbury had already put up a similar message. "I was astonished, utterly astonished, at the fact that another person was trying to start a club or a group of homebrewers," Mouer recalled. The two corralled eleven others and met at Stansbury's house on Park Avenue in February 1983. It wasn't until the following month that members picked a name—James River Homebrewers. The eventual motto of the group: "The art of brewing in the heart of Virginia."

A HISTORY OF BREWING IN THE RIVER CITY

The club's founding came just as the hobby was taking off. Only a few years earlier, homebrewing had been illegal—a quirk in the legacy of Prohibition and an odd circumstance for an activity dating to ancient times. As mentioned earlier, the domestic production of beer was born of necessity as much as recreation, particularly in the centuries leading to colonization of the New World. Settlers did not trust the water and turned to ale and cider to quench their thirsts. Our founding quaffers made sure someone among their household staff knew how to brew. Thomas Jefferson himself was an avid homebrewer, as was his wife, Martha. The ale brewed by their daughter, also named Martha, "was a treasured part of any visit to Monticello."

Jefferson provides two other important links to homebrewing heritage. One is a slave, Peter Hemings. A brother of Sally Hemings, he was trained by Joseph Miller, an English master brewer who had relocated to Virginia in 1813. Hemings learned not only to brew beer but also to malt barley, and once a brew house was built at Monticello, he experimented with making corn beer.

The other link is through a student at the University of Virginia—Mr. Jefferson's University. A young man named Charlie Papazian was studying nuclear engineering there in the early 1970s when a neighbor of a friend showed the gang an alternative to the cheap, tasteless beer they were buying.

"We went down in his basement, where he showed us some of his homebrew. He said, 'This is the good stuff,'" Papazian recalled. He was intrigued not only by the taste but also by the process. He decided to try his hand and scrounged together some bottles, bread yeast and cane sugar. "We ended up dumping the batch," he said with a grin during a visit to Richmond in 2000.

That might have been the only batch Papazian dumped. He later moved to Colorado, where he taught homebrewing. His instruction notes led to a book, *The Complete Joy of Homebrewing*, which hit the shelves in 1984. It wasn't the first homebrewing manual, but it was the most popular, going through several editions and eventually selling a million copies. Papazian went on to found the American Homebrewers Association, among other groups; he now is commonly regarded as the father of American homebrewing and one of the nation's seminal craft brewing figures. His refrain in the book ("Relax. Don't worry. Have a homebrew.") extended an affable invitation to join the fun.

The James River Homebrewers heard that message and put it into practice. Big Brew days for group brewing, club competitions and an active social calendar attracted increasing numbers to the point that meetings no longer fit comfortably in people's homes.

Anna Shore, elected president of the James River Homebrewers in 2014, participates in the 2013 Big Brew event. *Photo by Lee Graves.*

Sophistication was growing as well. Rob "Barley Bob" Barker, later the office manager for Legend Brewing Company, produced slick newsletters with articles about brewing techniques. Jim Dickerson, who later co-founded Commercial Taphouse & Grill, brought all-grain brewing skills to his role as president. "Homebrewers were certainly a part of the new beer revival of

Bob and Jeanne Henderson celebrated their twenty-fifth anniversary of operating the WeekEnd Brewer in Chester in 2013. *Photo by Lee Graves.*

the 1980s, and by the end of the decade much home-crafted beer was of professional quality," wrote award-winning homebrewer Jack Jackson in his history of the club.

One big boost for the scene was the emergence of a serious homebrew supply shop in Chester. Bob and Jeanne Henderson had met in junior high school and married while in high school. Their classmates voted them most likely not to succeed. That started to look prophetic when they could find only menial food-service jobs in California after high school.

In 1975, however, they moved to Virginia. Bob's skills repairing restaurant hardware led to a spot with Beverage Equipment Company, a supplier of kegs, taps, filters and other equipment. By 1987, the Hendersons owned the business, which had become a magnet for homebrewers; its location, however, in a cramped, lower-level space of a Chester building, was stifling.

"They called us the dungeon down there," Bob said in a 1998 interview. They moved to a larger upstairs layout in the same building in 1988, and soon the WeekEnd Brewer was a regional destination for specialty malts and hops. Homebrewers rejoiced—fresh supplies! And fresh energy. The Hendersons helped found a homebrewing club in Chester and pitched in at beer festivals in the village. (By the way—the shop celebrated its twenty-fifth anniversary in the same location in 2013, and at their twentieth high school reunion, the Hendersons learned they had been married the longest of any couple. So much for being least likely to succeed!)

The James River Homebrewers also found cause for rejoicing in another turn of events in 1993. Tom Martin, founder of Legend, pledged his support of the club in return for members' backing of the brewery. Legend's pub immediately became the adopted home of the group, and professional supplies became available when the brewery opened a small shop in its storage room. Between that and the WeekEnd Brewer, "We had access to the same malt and hops that the pros were using, and liquid yeast from Wyeast was the ingredient that made all the difference," Jack Jackson wrote. "The situation in the 1980s had been pitiful in this regard."

More homebrewers making better beers upped the ante for competitions, and the statewide Dominion Cup, birthed by the James River Homebrewers, provided a desirable trophy not only for individuals but for other clubs sprouting up in the region as well. Brewers like Rhett Rebold, Jeff Hewit, Frank Timmons, Lindsay Weiford, Tyler Kidd, Jean Korol, Anna and Ed Shore and Jackson made their marks in history with blue-ribbon beers.

Just as the microbrewing wave began to ebb in the late 1990s, homebrewing lost some of its devotees, both nationally and locally. Peaking at about a million participants in 1995, the hobby had dipped to roughly half that number when Papazian visited Richmond in 2000 on a tour to muster support and enthusiasm.

And just as craft brewing is now riding an even bigger wave, homebrewing is enjoying resurgence. The American Homebrewers Association estimates that there are more than 1 million homebrewers in the United States, and the ranks are swelling. "I would think [the growth rate] is more than 10 percent over the last few years, and it's probably closer to 20 percent," Gary Glass, director of the AHA, said in a 2013 interview. Attendance that year at the National Homebrewers Conference (rallying cry: "Brewing Up a Revolution") in Philadelphia set a record of 3,400 beer patriots.

It's not just numbers. There is more multi-generation family participation, more diversity and more women. "There's definitely a broader demographic in the hobby than there was ten years ago," Glass said. The wave of interest has spawned new clubs, such as Mentoring Advanced Standards of Homebrewing, and new businesses, such as Original Gravity homebrew supply store on Lakeside Avenue.

Original Gravity's owner Tony Ammendolia, came to Richmond for music, not homebrewing. An army brat, he grew up in several locations—Oklahoma,

Tony Ammendolia has established Original Gravity as a destination for homebrewers in North Richmond. *Photo by Lee Graves.*

Italy, Kentucky, northern Virginia—before attending Virginia Commonwealth University to study advertising.

"Really, I came for the music," Ammendolia said. When it became clear a career in music wasn't in the cards, he worked at food retail stores—Ellwood Thompson's Local Market and Whole Foods Market. In 1993, he was living with Dave Leon, and the two bought a homebrewing kit together. They created a brown ale from a recipe in Papazian's book, and they were hooked. Leon went on to become president of James River Homebrewers, and Ammendolia spent a decade crafting a business plan before opening Original Gravity in November 2011.

Both have seen the local scene blossom. The James River club now meets at Mekong Restaurant, and meetings are standing room only. Leon presided over the group's thirtieth-anniversary celebration, held at original sponsor Legend, and in early 2014, he passed the reins to Anna Shore, one of two women to lead the group (Korol was president in the late 1990s). "I think we've got a really strong community of homebrewers," Ammendolia said.

8

"THE TURNING POINT" FOR LOCAL BEER

On a muggy day in mid-May 2012, Governor Bob McDonnell met with a group of brewers, elected officials and industry representatives at Hardywood Park Craft Brewery. The air was thick with the bready-sweet smell of infant beer and the antiseptic zing of a freshly spiffed brew house. McDonnell shook hands, tasted some beer and then addressed the task at hand: signing legislation. House Bill 359, sponsored by Delegate Jennifer McLellan (D-Richmond, Henrico), allowed manufacturers to lease space in their brew houses to smaller brewers. Senate Bill 604, introduced by state senator Jeff McWaters (R-Virginia Beach), allowed retail sales of beer and sampling on brewery premises. The ceremony included putting together the ingredients for a special batch of brew: SB604 Special Bitter.

"Having everybody there, and collaborating, it was just a beautiful moment," recalled Brett Vassey, president and CEO of the Virginia Manufacturers Association. "It was exciting. It was the point in time where our entire industry points to and says, 'That was the turning point.'"

The impact, particularly of SB604, was immediate. Breweries became destinations. Tasting rooms became hip, with food trucks and live music. Small brewers could start on teeny systems and sell beer directly to customers, without having to go through a distributor. This maximized profits, streamlined the system and ensured fresh beer to patrons.

In Virginia, the number of operating breweries jumped from forty-two in 2012 to nearly ninety in mid-2014. Production among craft brewers leaped from 84,907 barrels to 129,103 barrels in 2013 (one barrel equals thirty-one U.S. gallons).

Richmond's scene also blossomed. Just as Hardywood was the setting for that moment, let's begin there for a rundown of the current brewing community and its evolution centuries after Christopher Newport and John Smith brought "beere" to RVA.

HARDYWOOD PARK CRAFT BREWERY

Eric McKay and Patrick Murtaugh spent a great deal of time and energy laying the foundation for Hardywood Park Craft Brewery. Identifying a receptive market, developing a solid business plan, networking with industry figures, honing their knowledge of brewing at top schools, nailing down the niche for their beers—all went into their thinking.

What they didn't think was "Let's brew a perfect beer." So when the Hardywood Park Reserve Series Gingerbread Stout received a score of one hundred out of one hundred in 2012 from *BeerAdvocate* magazine, well, it was more than a feather in the cap. "I would say it was arguably the most impactful credibility booster to our beer," McKay said.

"For someone as prolific as *BeerAdvocate* to say 'I don't see one single thing wrong with this beer' is pretty impressive, pretty cool to us," Murtaugh added.

That beer has received additional accolades and awards, as have other Hardywood beers. But just as the founders and head brewer Brian Nelson never set out to create a perfect beer, they don't devise recipes to win medals. Creativity motivates their brewing—being able to think outside the stylistic box, taking local ginger, hops, berries, pumpkins and even downed tulip poplar trees for original beers.

"We are intentionally brewing beers that don't fit style guidelines very well and, as a result, may not fare as well at competitions where they're judging how well it fits a style guideline," McKay said. "We hope that we can get people excited and experience flavors and aromas that they've never experienced before."

That said, Hardywood Singel, the brewery's flagship beer, is squarely in the box of widespread market appeal. The Belgian abbey-style blonde ale is mild and highly drinkable with enough spicy hop aroma and yeasty character to appeal to geeks and neophytes alike.

From left: Benjamin Petty, Patrick Murtaugh and Eric McKay of Hardywood Park Craft Brewery celebrate the release of Great Return IPA, named for the return of sturgeon to the James River. *Photo by Lee Graves.*

Friends since boyhood days in Connecticut, McKay and Murtaugh came to Richmond along a somewhat circuitous but well-explored path. In 2001, they were working in Australia on a sheep station, where the rancher brewed his own beer. The flavor made an impression, as did the location's name: Hardywood Park. They took up homebrewing and later worked as bartenders, as brewery apprentices and for a group of distributors in New York. Murtaugh studied at the Siebel Institute of Technology in Chicago and Doemens Academy in Munich, Germany; McKay excelled in marketing, got an MBA from Fordham and became a Certified Cicerone®. They looked around the country for the ideal place to plunk down their brewing boots. At a Craft Brewers Conference, they learned the Southeast was growing by three times the national average in craft beer volume but still had low market share. "We knew that from a portfolio standpoint, we wanted to brew beers that were a little more unique, more outside the box. So we were looking for a region that would appreciate creativity," McKay said.

It wasn't until McKay took a job with Specialty Beverage in Richmond that RVA began to appeal more than possibilities like Charlotte, North Carolina, which lacked a hometown brewery. The flourishing local restaurant scene, the strong artistic and cultural vibe and the sense of community in Richmond impressed them. "Ultimately, it took just being in Richmond to feel like this was the perfect place to start what we wanted to start," McKay said.

They found a warehouse on Ownby Lane within walking distance of the old Rosenegk brewery on Hermitage Road and set up a twenty-barrel system. When they opened in 2011, Legend was the only other viable craft brewery in town. Hardywood was an instant hit, not only in terms of beer but also as a hip destination for younger craft drinkers. Regular live and edgy music, a parking lot turned picnic spot with games for youngsters, food trucks with trendy fare, multiple taps in a barrel-bedecked brew house—Richmonders came in droves, particularly after the passage of Senate Bill 604. In 2013, the operation expanded into an adjacent building to accommodate another tasting room and offices. Production that year was 4,300 barrels. By mid-2014, Hardywood's beers were being distributed in northern Virginia and Washington, D.C., as well.

As much as Richmonders have embraced Hardywood, the team has reached out to the community. Hardywood's first canned beer, a cream ale, pays homage to the historic 1935 worldwide debut of canned beer in the city. The RVA IPA bears the fruit of a two-way project—giving away hop rhizomes to growers who donate the results back for use in the beer. The Great Return, a West Coast IPA, celebrates the resurgence of endangered Atlantic sturgeon in the James River and provides donations to the James River Association.

McKay and Murtaugh aren't the only ones who found brewing passion on the other side of the world. Nelson gave up an R&D job with Honda in

Ohio to move with his wife to New Zealand. He'd been homebrewing while in the States, and at Galbraith's Alehouse in Auckland, he landed a spot as assistant brewer. "It was there I learned to appreciate the process of making great beer, not just beer," he says on his blog.

"Stay balanced, keep moving" is Nelson's motto. Not a bad one for Hardywood as a whole.

LEGEND BREWING COMPANY

I'm sitting on the deck of Legend, drinking a cold Tripel on a hot summer day and admiring a view that was only a vision in Tom Martin's head two decades ago.

Now, a row of locust, pine and other trees partially obscures the rail cars and concrete pads of Manchester's industrial heart. The eye jumps to the city's floodwall, where a runner in a fluorescent yellow T-shirt jogs in the July heat. Then to the James River as it flows among rocks, coursing beneath and beyond the Manchester Bridge. Finally, to Richmond's skyline, buildings old and new stacked in the air like Legos, modestly majestic, as befits a state capital of midsize ambitions.

Martin had a somewhat different view in the winter of 1992–93. He had already investigated several other sites for his brewery, including Main Street Station and the former warehouse in Shockoe Slip that eventually housed the Richbrau brewpub. But the South Side site caught his eye. Only a portion of the building was for rent at the time, and trash, scrub trees and rusting equipment blighted the surroundings. Still, Martin recalled, "I stood there as the sun was going down one winter day and watched the sun reflect off the city and said, 'Man, this is a really nice view here. If we can get it, it would be really good.'"

It has been good, on many levels. Legend has survived where others microbreweries have failed. Legend Brown Ale has become an iconic brew among Central Virginia's beer lovers. And the deck has become a fixture for those seeking a brew with a view.

One thing Martin could not have envisioned was the hothouse blossoming of beer culture in the region. From being the city's lone brewery in 2010, Legend has watched the number of breweries climb into double digits in the metro area and the number of craft beer styles go into the stratosphere. On this day, as I sit typing, Strangeways is celebrating its one-year anniversary with three new beers, Hardywood Park is releasing its Virginia Blackberry Belgian-style White Ale, Lickinghole Creek is releasing its Batchelors Delight Rum Barrel Belgian-style Quadrupel Ale and Triple Crossing is unveiling Street Cred, an IPA collaboration with the Answer Brewpub.

Martin welcomes the diversity. "I think competition is good. It keeps everybody on their toes and gets the creativity flowing," he said. "The trouble with doing different beers every day is, for us we can't do that. We need to make beers that are consistent that we can sell into the market, that people will continue to buy, and put on tap, and keep on tap so that we can continue to grow."

Actually, Martin chuckles about the pace of Legend's growth. In 2013, production was about twelve thousand barrels, "which in twenty years is amazingly slow growth. It is what it is. We're still alive, and that's a good thing."

As mentioned earlier (see Chapter 6), Legend started with four recipes—Legend Brown, Legend Lager, Legend Pilsner and Legend Porter—that Martin developed in consultation with his father. Solid, no-frills, straightforward beers in twenty-two-ounce bottles defined the brewery in its early years, and consistently well-made seasonals and flagship brews buoyed its survival. The new wave of breweries and the proliferation of offerings, however, changed the landscape.

"When we started out, just making good beer was enough…We're trying to find our way in all of that," said Dave Gott, vice-president of operations, in a 2013 interview. "The goal for us is staying true to what we've always done but not get left behind in this frenzy of new, exotic beers."

The Urban Legend series was launched in 2013 as a means to pump fresh creative juices into the offerings and the image. Four specialty beers were packaged with stories—"legends," if you will—about Richmond's past. They ranged from a doppelbock celebrating a statue of a beloved black dog to a red ale evoking tales of a vampire-like figure that emerged from the ruins of a tunnel that had collapsed on a train. The second installment of the series involved collaborations with other state breweries and legends—an oyster stout made with Hampton's St. George Brewing Company and paired with the story of the notorious pirate Blackbeard, for example.

The backbone of Legend's success, however, has been its Brown Ale. As Legend beers have moved into high-volume retail accounts such as Walmart and Costco, the Brown Ale has accounted for 60 to 65 percent of overall sales, Gott said. It's also a star in Brown Distributing Company's portfolio. "No other brown ale from any other company has come close," said Jacob Brunow, Brown's craft and import director. That includes browns from Newcastle, Smuttynose, Avery—even an Olde Richmond Brown "brought in and contracted for years out of Richmond just to try and battle Legend."

Stylistically, Legend Brown Ale lands between definitive English brown ales—the hoppier, nuttier ales to the north and the sweeter, maltier browns to the south. Caramel and roasted barley malts account for two prominent aspects of the profile. Two-row pale malt provides the base of the grain bill, and Briess Extra Special Malt adds depth and a "raisin" quality, said head brewer John Wampler. The yeast is the 1056 "Chico" strain, which is "clean and fruity and brings out the malt character."

For hops, Wampler uses Columbus for bittering and Willamette for flavoring and aroma. Ingredients have been juggled now and then. Mount Hood hops, for example, were used instead of Willamette in early batches. "Like any good brewer, we've made efforts to improve without changing a good beer," Wampler said.

For the brewery's twentieth-anniversary celebration—a boisterous affair with bagpipes, proclamations by elected officials and enthusiastic support from Richmond's beer-loving community—the Brown Ale got special treatment. Wampler and his co-brewers made an imperial version using seven types of malt and more hops for a robust ale weighing in at 8.3 percent alcohol by volume.

Legend now owns the building it rented for so many years, which makes planning for growth easier, Martin said. But it doesn't necessarily ensure security. "I've always been afraid of going out of business—still am. I always have too much worry. I should just...not worry," he said and laughed. Juggling priorities between the brewery and the restaurant has fed some of those anxieties.

Would he do it all over again? "Yes, but not this way. I'd start with a lot more money and do something on the level of Devils Backbone," he said. That brewery started with a "basecamp" brewpub in Nelson County and then expanded in 2011 to an "outpost" production facility in Lexington that involved a $6 million investment and a goal of producing forty thousand to fifty thousand barrels in 2014.

Ventures like that keep an element of optimism in Martin's vision. "I hope the craft brewery segment continues to grow so that it allows everybody to grow," he said. "We still need to grow."

MIDNIGHT BREWERY

Trae Cairns noticed a pattern in his homebrewing. After putting out fires in his IT job at Estes Express Lines; after spending time with his wife, Debra, and tucking in his daughter, Alexis; after tending to all other domestic chores, he was able to hunker down to beer chores—washing bottles, starting yeast cultures, tweaking recipes.

"I made mention of it to a co-worker, that it was always midnight when I finished," Cairns said. The reference stuck. "I'm the Midnight Brewer—and that's how it started."

Midnight Brewery was a vision for Cairns, however, long before the doors opened in 2012. As with many others, a Mr. Beer homebrew kit from his wife kindled his interest, but his passion for doing something different had been building for years.

A Henrico County native, Cairns spent a couple of years at Virginia Commonwealth University after graduation from J.R. Tucker High School and then earned a degree in administration of justice from J. Sargeant Reynolds Community College. Law enforcement had been his goal, but the telephone industry called. A series of jobs and layoffs made for an

Becky Rudolf is lead brewer, but the brewing chores are shared with Trae Cairns, owner, at Midnight Brewery. *Photo by Lee Graves.*

unsettling stretch in his twenties, and the instability kept him from investing in homebrewing, a hobby that appealed to him.

"Cooking is something I enjoy, and I thought homebrewing would be similar," Cairns said. Seven years before going pro, he brewed his first batch. Soon, he was consumed. "My family was tired of me talking about beer." Debra, who disliked the smell of brewing, kicked him out of the kitchen but supported his growing ambition. At dinner one night in 2010, he broached the idea of going commercial. "She was very supportive; then she asked, 'How do you open a brewery?' I gave her that deer-in-headlights look and said, 'I have no idea.' I hadn't thought about it."

Cairns took a course at the Siebel Institute of Technology in Chicago. As his plans took shape, he decided to finance the endeavor himself rather than go through investors. "Most of them want a return on their money, and there's nothing wrong with that," Cairns said. "I didn't want to be forced into pushing things."

His first batch was a collaboration: Banana Pancakes (a wheat beer with esters giving the banana profile, plus maple syrup from Highland County, Virginia) brewed with Hardywood in March 2012. Midnight officially opened its tasting room doors that May. Brewing quickly expanded from a 1.5-barrel system to 3.0 barrels, and in March 2014, Cairns took another step. Construction began on a 5,400-square-foot facility that features a new tasting room, a 10.0-barrel brewing setup and 20.0-barrel fermenters, all purchased from O'Connor Brewing Company in Norfolk. Production reached 250.0 barrels in 2013, and Becky Rudolf has taken a role as lead brewer.

She and Cairns share a similar philosophy. "I want beers that anybody can come in here and drink, whether it's the kölsch or the oatmeal stout," Rudolf said. "I want to brew what a regular person can come in and enjoy."

Like many breweries, Midnight is tucked away in an industrial park, the Rockville Commerce Center off state Route 623 in Goochland County. Live music and food trucks help draw crowds for special events, such as the release of one of the trademark seasonals, Christmas at Midnight. The initial tasting room reflected Cairns's personality—easygoing, approachable and personable.

"When I designed the tasting room, I had one design in mind," Cairns said. "I wanted the atmosphere to feel like your back porch, where good friends come over and sit around and drink great beer. Telling stories and catching up with one another. I did not have the intent to make it a bar. I wanted families to feel good about bringing their kids as well. We are not kid-friendly but kid-tolerable."

Midnight's bestseller is Rockville Red, an Irish-style red made with Maris Otter and three other malts with East Kent Golding hops (5.5 percent ABV). Cairns has also had great success establishing the brewery's New Beginning Kölsch—brewed with pilsner and Vienna malts and Hallertau hops—as a gateway beer. Mainstream quaffers take to its light drinkability (5.6 percent ABV) and full flavor.

Other flagship beers include the Not My Job Brown Ale, using an assertive hop blend of East Kent Golding, Liberty and Willamette hops, at 5 percent ABV, and Head First Pale Ale, featuring pale and Munich malts with Cascade and Citra hops. In June 2014, the brewery released Virginia Midway, a wheat beer brewed specifically for the State Fair of Virginia.

Just as Cairns got help from McKay and Murtaugh at Hardywood, he has passed along his insights to other brewers just starting out. Mike Isley, owner of Isley Brewing Company in Scott's Addition, praised Cairns in particular for his aid. That reflects an atmosphere that permeates the Richmond scene. "I think this is a great group right now of brewers and brewery owners," Cairns said. "There's not a person out there that I couldn't reach out to to get an answer, an honest answer, if I had a question."

CENTER OF THE UNIVERSE BREWING COMPANY

Chris and Phil Ray could hardly have started down more different career paths. Chris followed an outstanding collegiate baseball career at the College of William and Mary with success in Major League Baseball. Drafted in the third round, he played for the Baltimore Orioles and several other teams, including the 2010 World Series champion San Francisco Giants. Phil used a master's degree in mechanical engineering from the University of South Florida to land a job with Honeywell in Florida. Though Phil worked with satellite technology and guidance systems, brewing beer was not on his radar.

That is, not until Chris started homebrewing between games while pitching in the minors for the Orioles. "I called Phil and asked him if I bought him a homebrew kit, would he use it," Chris said. "He said yes, so I sent him one down to Tampa, and it kind of snowballed from there."

The passion grew while Chris was pitching in Seattle and San Francisco, two major beer-loving cities. The West Coast scene opened Chris's eyes to the potential in the Richmond area. "In Seattle, there's a hundred breweries

Phil Ray (left) and his brother, Chris, opened Center of the Universe Brewing Company in Ashland in November 2012. *Photo by Lee Graves.*

in a hundred-mile radius." Phil chimed in. "And in Seattle, craft beer is 30 percent of the beer market there, and 90 percent of that is local."

The "local is good" philosophy has served the Rays well. They borrowed the brewery's name from the "center of the universe" slogan of Ashland, where Chris lives with his wife, Alice (a Hanover County native), and their daughter and son. The town has returned the love and been supportive since COTU opened in the fall of 2012. "Every single day, literally, five or six people will come up to us and thank us for opening," Phil says.

Head brewer Mike Killelea has helped fashion a cross-section of beers: Ray Ray's Pale Ale, rich with citrusy Cascade hops balanced by English two-row barley; Main St. Virginia ale, an easy-drinking alt style; Pocahoptas IPA, which uses four varieties of Pacific Northwest hops; and one-off brews ranging from an imperial IPA to a German kölsch. COTU's tasting room reflects the green and gold of William and Mary's colors, and picnic tables and a stage for live music outside create a family-friendly atmosphere.

Like other brewers in the area, the Rays and Killelea have been heavily involved in community and charity programs. One outreach program extends back to Chris's days in Seattle and his interest in Operation Homefront, a charity that helps military veterans and their families. The brothers teamed with Fremont Brewing Company in Seattle to produce Homefront IPA, which is aged on Louisville Slugger maple bats. Since its launch in 2011, the annual program has raised hundreds of thousands of dollars and involved a dozen or so breweries across the country.

That collaboration led to a partnership with Richmond's minor-league baseball team, the Flying Squirrels. A Vienna-style amber lager named Chin Music—the term refers to high, tight pitches meant to send a message to an opposing batter—was brewed in early 2014 for release as a year-round beer and a stadium special for the Flying Squirrels.

Coming up with new recipes is a team effort among the brothers and Killelea. "The three of us all have a similar approach to beers," Phil says. "We understand we're not brewing only to homebrewers here. We know we need to appeal to a broad spectrum of beer drinkers."

That hasn't constrained their creativity. El Duderino, for example, plays off the Coen brothers' movie *The Big Lebowski*, where bowling and white Russians in the film inspire the beer's graphic design and the ingredients of the white Russian milk stout.

On the less wacky side, 2014 found them re-releasing Scotchtown Ale, a Scottish-style beer using eight malts, including roasted barley and smoked malt. Just as Pocahoptas is a nod to the story of Pocahontas, Scotchtown Ale pays tribute to the one-time Hanover County home of Patrick Henry, the orator of "Give Me Liberty or Give Me Death" fame. "I think we've found our groove going with history," Phil said. "There's so much history here in Richmond."

STRANGEWAYS BREWING

Walk into Strangeways Brewing on Dabney Road, and you know you're not in Kansas anymore. You are greeted by a portrait of a chimpanzee, mysteriously nicknamed AFM. A boar's head wearing a fez looks down on the bar. Curios such as bottle racks made of recycled wooden barrels and metal gears line the walls. Photos, logos and knickknacks of brewing trivia lie beneath plate glass on the counter, as if in a museum display case.

You begin to understand the brewery's motto: "Think strange. Drink strange." And indeed, the beers fit the quirky ambience created by owner Neil Burton and sustained by brewer Mike Hiller. Flagship brews include Woodbooger, a Belgian-style brown ale that plays off the nickname for

Neil Burton, owner of Strangeways Brewing, celebrates the release of OTIS Cucumber Melon Sour with his wife, Maya Eckstein. *Photo by Lee Graves.*

Virginia's version of Bigfoot; Albino Monkey, a white ale brewed with spices; Phantasmic East Coast IPA, a seventy-IBU piney, fruity alternative to the West Coast style; and recent additions Wild Wallonian Dawn and Überlin Berliner Weiss.

Since the brewery's opening in the spring of 2013, a portfolio of sours and bocks, including an ice bock, has added flair to the offerings. The brewing envelope is stretched further with Strangeways' regular Compendium of Curiosities, where the standard lineup gets twisted with infusions of exotica—teas, fruits and berries, wet hops, jasmine and other adventurous ingredients.

"Neil has pretty much given us carte blanche. We've got the capacity to brew any kind of beer we want to," said Hiller, standing amid the gleaming array of tanks in their twenty-barrel system. Burton added, "We want to approach it from a creative standpoint rather than to find a particular niche in the marketplace."

Strangeways' debut crowned four years of effort—it was Burton's full-time job for two years. His passion for beer stretches further, to a college semester abroad (he hails from Fredericksburg but is a Wake Forest Demon Deacon). On his way to Austria to study international business, he landed in Munich during Oktoberfest. "At the time, I was not a beer drinker. I didn't like American beer," Burton said. "That experience abroad opened a whole new world to me."

He developed a business plan that initially focused on using other breweries' equipment to produce his own beers, a common practice through contract brewing and alternative proprietorship arrangements. Virginia laws proved a stumbling block, however, so he worked with lawyers, lawmakers, brewers and distributors on enabling legislation. At the bill's signing ceremony, he met Hiller. "Mike and I instantly hit it off," said Burton. "I liked Mike's unique background and the beers he had produced and wanted to produce."

Hiller was a familiar face in brewing circles through several years of work at Legend Brewing in Richmond and later operating his own brewery, Bavarian Barbarian, in Pennsylvania. He closed that operation and went to Cabinet Artisanal Brewhouse in Alexandria.

Burton's vision, which had evolved from using others' equipment to building his own brewery, lured Hiller to Strangeways. Their emphasis has been on developing a production facility, with bottles, kegs and cans distributed by Brown Distributing, in addition to a tasting room for in-house draft lovers.

Perhaps more than any other Richmond brewery, Strangeways has secured a niche and an identity. From the unique twenty-five or so beers on tap in the multiple tasting rooms to the offbeat décor of the 8,400-square-foot facility—even the company's name reflects a direction outside the mainstream. It combines Burton's love for the English alternative rock group The Smiths (their final studio album was *Strangeways, Here We Come*) and his sense of how his career path was taking an unusual turn, from the family's clothing business to brewing.

"The name 'Strangeways' also represents the unusual beers we plan to brew," Burton added in a 2013 interview. "We also see how it relates to individualism—how people are unique in ways that others may perceive as odd or...strange. And we want to celebrate people's strangeness."

One of the stranger experiments during the first year was Hiller's Freeze Ray Eisbock, a follow-up to the Mixolydian Rag Rye Bock and Blitzkrieg Bock Schwarzbock in the bock program. He and Burton have made their mark as well with sours, particularly using lactobacillus. The bacteria, like yeast, metabolize sugars as a source of energy, but unlike yeast, they produce lactic acid instead of alcohol. Kiss Off! Cherry Sour (Burton also is a fan of the band Kiss), Word! Sour Saison and Whap! Sorachi Sour all have delivered mouth-puckering power derived from lactobacillus. The brewery also makes good use of the Brettanomyces yeast with Überlin Berliner Weiss and Wake Me Up Before You Gose.

Even the celebration of spring's annual rite of basketball frenzy took a Strangeways twist. A March Hop Madness featured a Sweet Sixteen of hoppy beers, including the release of Houblonic Belgian IPA. If you can guess the derivation of "houblonic," you probably also can guess what AFM stands for.

LICKINGHOLE CREEK CRAFT BREWERY

Goochland County is known as horse country, its rolling hills and Piedmont pastures dotted with sturdy barns and riding rinks. So the design of Lickinghole Creek's brewery, a white stable-like building sitting on a commanding knoll, fits in with the farmland.

The fit goes beyond appearances. Lickinghole Creek fills a niche in the area's brewing scene that emphasizes agriculture—grow it yourself, if possible, or use local ingredients if they're available. The 260-acre property sports hop vines, pumpkin patches, blackberry and raspberry thickets, a sophisticated water treatment-reclamation system and the beginnings of

The Pumphreys grow Columbus and several other varieties of hops as part of the agricultural aspect of Lickinghole Creek's farm brewery. *Photo by Lee Graves.*

grain fields, all with the ambition of establishing a terroir for its beers and a rural, breath-of-fresh-air destination for beer lovers.

"It's unique in craft brewing in Virginia," said Sean-Thomas Pumphrey, who began the venture with his wife, Lisa. "It's like a winery and craft brewing combined."

Pumphrey began growing hops at the farm "before we had any inclination of having a brewery out here." He had discovered craft beer in the shape of Moose Drool Brown Ale and its kin while a student at the University of Montana. Homebrewing came next, and the hop fields followed. On a blistering day in 2013, he reached into a Columbus plant—the most lush among more than one thousand vines and a dozen varieties—pulled out a few cones and rolled them in his hands to release the rich, piney aroma. He smiled with the pride of a red-clay farmer.

That passion is shared. "I tilled the soil myself for the pumpkins," said Farris Loutfi, a co-founder and sidekick of Pumphrey's going back to Henrico County high school days and University of Richmond grad school. Loutfi provides mechanical and troubleshooting savvy and is "the face of the tasting room and a personality many of our customers and clients seek out," said Lisa.

The head brewing responsibilities on the twenty-barrel system rest with David Achkio, an alumnus of the Siebel Institute of Technology and former brewer with Pyramid Breweries on the West Coast and Blue & Gray Brewing Company in Fredericksburg.

As CEO of the operation, Lisa handles most of the business matters; she also works with legislators, distributors and state regulatory agencies. "She makes it all happen. You want something done, you give it to her and it will get done," Sean said.

Their stable of beers includes Three Chopt Tripel Ale, which uses Belgian pilsner malt, Belgian yeast and Sterling and New Zealand Motueka hops for a brew weighing in at 9.3 percent ABV and thirty-nine IBUs. (A bourbon barrel–aged version of the Tripel received rave reviews in the beer media.) "On the hops, we're generally on the edge of stylistic guidelines with our beers," Pumphrey said.

Short Pump Saison, a farmhouse ale, has Galena, Columbus and Nugget hops, plus two types of rye, along with the barley for a 6.8 percent ABV brew. Magic Beaver Belgian-style Pale Ale is hopped with American and New Zealand varieties for thirty IBUs and 5.5 percent ABV. Gentleman Farmer Estate Hop Ale—a limited-release batch—boasted four varieties of

Lisa Pumphrey (second from right), co-founder of Lickinghole Creek Craft Brewery, talks about the farm brewery operation during the 2014 Capital Ale House National Beer Expo. *Photo by Lee Graves.*

The James River Steam Brewery caves at Rocketts Landing were added to the National Register of Historic Places in 2014. *Photo by Chris Johnson.*

The Peter Stumpf Brewing Company at Harrison and Clay Streets was notable not only for its production capacity but also for the beer garden (at back) and eagle logo (bottom left corner). *Valentine Richmond History Center.*

Left: A post-Prohibition Richbrau beer can, on display at Devils Backbone Brewing Company Basecamp in Nelson County. *Photo by Lee Graves.*

Below: Tom Martin (left), founder of Legend Brewing Company, points out parts of the brewery to former governor Bob McDonnell and his wife, Maureen, during the twentieth-anniversary celebration. *Photo by Lee Graves.*

Rick Ivey tends to some of the Cascade hops growing on Rusty Beaver Brewery's farm near the Ladysmith tasting room. *Photo by Lee Graves.*

Becky Hammond brews a batch of beer at the Short Pump location of Rock Bottom Restaurant and Brewery, which opened in June 2014. *Photo by Lee Graves.*

Above: Founder Steve Crandall (far left), head brewer Jason Oliver (second from left) and other Devils Backbone employees celebrate winning the 2013 Virginia Brewers Cup Best of Show award. *Photo by Lee Graves.*

Left: The Peter Stumpf Brewing Company started originally as the Richmond Brewing Company and later changed its named to Home Brewing Company. *Photo by Jennifer Pullinger.*

Like many of the Hardywood Park Reserve Series beers, the Virginia Blackberry is made with ingredients from local sources. *Photo by Jennifer Pullinger.*

The crew at Legend Brewing Company includes founder Tom Martin (standing, third from right) and head brewer John Wampler (to Martin's left). *Photo by Jennifer Pullinger.*

Left: Hops are put to good advantage in brews such as Pocahoptas IPA at Center of the Universe Brewing Company in Ashland. *Photo by Jennifer Pullinger.*

Below: Becky Rudolf has put her signature touch on Purdy Mechanic IPA and many other beers at Midnight Brewery. *Photo by Jennifer Pullinger.*

Head brewer David Achkio (background) monitors the operation as bottles of Pony Pasture Pilsner are filled at Lickinghole Creek Craft Brewery. *Photo by Jennifer Pullinger.*

In the spring of 2014, brewer Dylan Brooks (left) joined the family operation headed by Judy and Jason Harr at Extra Billy's Smokehouse and Brewery in Midlothian. *Photo by Jennifer Pullinger.*

Right: Jeremy Wirtes checks the status of a batch at Triple Crossing Brewing Company as Brandon Tolbert (background) of the Answer Brewpub looks on. *Photo by Jennifer Pullinger.*

Opposite top, left: Sean-Thomas Pumphrey checks out some of the hops growing at Lickinghole Creek Craft Brewery, a farm brewery in Goochland County. *Photo by Jennifer Pullinger.*

Opposite top, right: AFM, the mascot at Strangeways Brewing, is only one of the curiosities adding flavor to the tasting areas. *Photo by Jennifer Pullinger.*

Opposite bottom: Mike Hiller, head brewer at Strangeways Brewing, samples one of the barrel-aged beers. Strangeways has made a mark with its sour beers and bocks as well. *Photo by Jennifer Pullinger.*

Left: Rock Bottom Restaurant and Brewery opened its first location in six years in June 2014 at Short Pump Town Center. *Photo by Jennifer Pullinger.*

Below: The leading figures at the Answer Brewpub are An Bui, owner; Brandon Tolbert, brewer; and April Herrington, general manager. *Photo by Jennifer Pullinger.*

Right: Kevin O'Leary was a brewer at Cambridge Brewing Company in Massachusetts before joining Paul Karns and Tom Sullivan to form Ardent Craft Ales. *Photo by Jennifer Pullinger.*

Below: Rick Ivey (left) and his son, Austin, teamed up to form Rusty Beaver Brewery in Ladysmith. *Photo by Lee Graves.*

Above: The team at Isley Brewing Company includes head brewer Josh Stamps, assistant brewer Aaron Lile and owner Mike Isley. *Photo by Jennifer Pullinger.*

Left: Bob and Jeanne Henderson of the WeekEnd Brewer in Chester have been central figures in the Richmond homebrewing scene. *Photo by Jennifer Pullinger.*

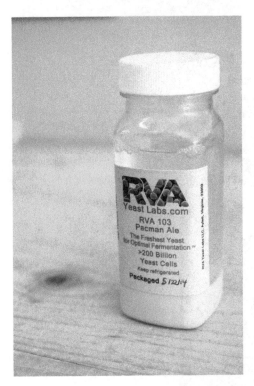

Jason Ridlon and Malachy McKenna, veteran homebrewers, founded RVA Yeast Labs in December 2013. *Photo by Jennifer Pullinger.*

In addition to making Original Gravity a destination on Lakeside Avenue, Tony Ammendolia collaborated with Isley Brewing Company to produce Venus Flytrap IPA. *Photo by Jennifer Pullinger.*

Left: James Talley, regarded by some as the godfather of craft beer in Richmond, opened Commercial Taphouse & Grill with Jim Dickerson in 1993. *Photo by Jennifer Pullinger.*

Opposite top: Terry O'Neill (left), founder of Penny Lane Pub, and son Terence have kept the place jumping since relocating to Fifth Street in 2003. *Photo by Jennifer Pullinger.*

Opposite bottom, left: British pride is evident at Penny Lane Pub, where Beatles memorabilia is a reminder of founder Terry O'Neill's friendship with the Liverpool band's members. *Photo by Jennifer Pullinger.*

Opposite bottom, right: Members of the River City Beer Betties gather for a brew at Ardent Craft Ales in Scott's Addition. *Photo by Jennifer Pullinger.*

Chris Holder (left) and Matthew Simmons have grown Capital Ale House from its original location on Main Street in downtown Richmond to five sites statewide. *Photo by Jennifer Pullinger.*

It's common at Mekong Restaurant to see local breweries, such as Ashland's Center of the Universe, sharing tap space with more exotic beers. *Photo by Jennifer Pullinger.*

hops grown on the farm. "[It is] our attempt to add terroir (the taste of place) to beer," the brewery's website reads.

In August 2013, Lickinghole paired with Midnight for an all-Goochland collaboration, Generator-X. The Belgian-style ale got its name when a generator came to the rescue after a power outage (ironically, it rained like hell and threatened another outage at the release party).

Though the brewery is a good forty-five-minute ride from downtown Richmond, Lickinghole has had enthusiastic turnouts for events, such as its grand opening in September 2013 and a rollicking release of its Enlightened Despot, a Russian Imperial Stout, at a mansion in Goochland County.

The Pumphreys have played a central role in forwarding the concept of farm breweries in Virginia. They worked with Goochland County officials as they revamped zoning ordinances to establish a farm brewery designation, and in 2014, the Virginia General Assembly passed legislation that intends to put farm breweries on a more equal footing with the state's wineries.

One of the main reasons for starting the brewery, Lisa said, "was a dream of creating a viable agricultural business model that would encourage the conservation of open space, wildlife habitat, promote agriculture and encourage the public to embrace and play in the outdoors."

ISLEY BREWING COMPANY

The opening of Isley Brewing Company in October 2013 provided a connect-the-dots moment for Richmond's beer community. Remember the Rosenegk and Home Brewing companies from pre-Prohibition days? Isley's location in Scott's Addition puts that history within a few minutes' drive for beer geeks who appreciate the past.

Isley also put a third craft beer destination within easy traveling distance for those looking to maximize tasting opportunities while minimizing driving. Now, with Ardent Craft Ales also in Scott's Addition, a string of distinctive breweries—count Strangeways on Dabney Road and Hardywood Park on Ownby Lane—spreads like a welcome mat to Richmond's brewing scene. On the south side of Broad Street, Triple Crossing and Legend continue the string inside the city limits.

Isley's debut was a moment to savor. Within earshot, crowds partied along the Boulevard during the Pumpkin Festival. A band of beer explorers filed into the brewery's spacious ocher-and-brick tasting room as soon as the doors

ABC MANAGERS	'THE BRIBE'	6.6% ABV	12 oz	GROWLER
AARON THACKERY	OATMEAL PORTER	19 IBU		32 oz/64 oz
JOSH STAMPS			$5	$8/15
ALEXANDRA TILBE	'BETWIXT'	5.5% ABV		
ALSO FOR SALE...	AMERICAN PALE ALE	70 IBU	$5	$8/15
Chips $2	'PLAIN JANE'	5.4% ABV		
Daddy G's Salsa $5	BELGIAN WHITE ALE	16 IBU	$5	$8/15
Soda $1	'ROOT OF ALL EVIL'	5.9% ABV		
Isley Tshirts $20	GINGER Golden Ale	14 IBU	$5	$8/15
	'PARADIGM' [INFUSION]	5.5% ABV		
	PEAR INFUSION OF BETWIXT APA	70 IBU	$6	$9/18
GROWLERS $7 64 oz TO TAKE HOME	'CHOOSY MOTHER' ON NITRO	6.6 ABV		
Sold Out	PEANUT BUTTER OATMEAL PORTER	19 IBU	$7	N/A

Isley Brewing Company opened its tasting room in Scott's Addition in October 2013. *Photo by Lee Graves.*

opened. On tap were the two flagship beers—Plain Jane Belgian White Ale and the Bribe Oatmeal Porter—and their cousins, Plain Jane Blueberry Belgian White Ale and Decadence Coconut Cocoa Oatmeal Porter.

The Bribe—chewy and complex, yet silky smooth from the oats—connects with the backgrounds of Josh Stamps, Isley's head brewer, and Aaron Thackery, former brewery manager. Friends since youth and homebrewing sidekicks for years, they won gold at the 2012 Dominion Cup competition with their oak-aged oatmeal stout.

Isley has added Betwixt, an American Pale Ale notable for its German hops and sessionable 5.5 percent ABV. Also, they've shown creative flash with infusions of their flagship beers, such as Choosy Mother Peanut Butter Oatmeal Porter and Up All Night Coffee Oatmeal Porter. As of this writing, they're brewing on a three-barrel system, with seven-barrel tanks for fermenting and conditioning.

Owner Mike Isley estimated that they would brew 750 barrels the first year, all for draft consumption rather than bottles or cans. "I don't want to be a mass producer of beer," Isley said. "I just want to make really good beer."

In addition to heading up the brewery, Isley runs the family business, Winter Plumbing and Heating. He experienced another connect-the-dots feeling when beginning upgrades to the building. It was his company that installed the original plumbing back in 1920. He credits other Richmond-area brewers—Trae Cairns at Midnight in Goochland, Neil Burton at Strangeways, Eric McKay and Patrick Murtaugh at Hardywood—with pitching in to help the brewery get up and running. "They definitely practice what they preach when it comes to camaraderie in the business," Isley said.

TRIPLE CROSSING BREWING COMPANY

Triple Crossing's debut marked a surge of brewery openings in the spring of 2014. While it gained advantage from the booming beer culture in Richmond, the brewery faced a familiar challenge: distinguishing itself from others.

One distinction rests on the Foushee Street location—it's within walking distance of college facilities, on the way home for many downtown commuters and in a historic building that was attractively rebuilt with exposed brick, steel beams and a patio. Another element giving Triple Crossing identity is its name. On one level, the name refers to a renowned spot about a mile to the southeast, where three railroad lines cross vertically. It's the only such crossing in the world, according to several sources.

But the name also alludes to the connection binding the brewery's trio of founding co-owners—Scott Jones, Adam Worcester and head brewer Jeremy Wirtes. Jones and Worcester have been friends since childhood, growing up in the Smoketree area of Chesterfield County, going through the same public schools and later fostering a passion for good beer. Wirtes, originally from Newport News, moved to Chesterfield in 2005, and the three immediately plugged into a shared vision when they sat down together at Sedona Taphouse in October 2012.

Priorities from the get-go were transparency about what they're brewing and community involvement in where they're going. The tanks, including four seven-barrel fermentation tanks and five seven-barrel bright tanks, are visible in the tasting room. The brewer's blog gives insights into what's going on behind the scenes, and a digital screen above the bar spells out profiles and invites comments.

"This place could be like a forum for what people think about recipes or styles," Wirtes said before their opening. "For us, it's like a big testing

Triple Crossing's name partly refers to the friendship of (from left) Jeremy Wirtes, Scott Jones and Adam Worcester. *Photo by Lee Graves.*

ground, for lack of a better word. We can make what beers we want—and we will—but we also want to know what people want."

"We have ideas, but we don't know what it's going to turn into," Jones said.

Those ideas, in terms of the beer, are pretty straightforward—hoppy beers with a focus on historic English styles. "There's a mantra that I like: Complicated is not good, but complex is," Wirtes said. "That's how we do things around here. I really like simple, clean flavors in our beers."

Falcon Smash, an India Pale Ale, was an early offering intended to help establish the brewery's identity. It was double dry-hopped using predominantly Falconer's Flight (a Pacific Northwest hop) for flavor and bitterness and Motueka (a New Zealand variety) for aroma.

In terms of that identity, Triple Crossing wants to be a destination for RVA hopheads. If you're not a hophead, though, don't despair. Element 79 (hint: think the periodic table) is modeled after a British Golden Ale, lighter and more accessible than Falcon Smash with an ABV of about 4.5 percent. Geeks will appreciate that it's brewed with a single hop (Palisade), a single malt (pale ale malt) and an atypical yeast (WLP002).

"English beers today—some of the bigger brands—are seen as more subtle than their American counterparts. But English beers back then were anything but. They were just as strong then as they are today on the West Coast," Wirtes said. "That's the kind of thing we're going to do a lot of."

As a stamp of validation on its approach and its beers, Triple Crossing received three medals its first year at the 2014 Virginia Craft Brewers Fest.

ARDENT CRAFT ALES

Isley Brewing Company put a pin on Richmond's beer map. The opening of Ardent Craft Ales on Leigh Street put a question mark: what the heck is going on in Scott's Addition?

The answer combines a bit of history with a bunch of promise. Named after General Winfield Scott, the commanding general of the U.S. Army in the 1800s, the plot was annexed by the city in 1914. Scott, whose nickname was "Old Fuss and Feathers," was the son-in-law of Colonel John Mayo and one of the ablest men of his time. Ardent's debut in June 2014 followed Isley's launch on Summit Avenue the previous fall. Another venture, Black Heath Meadery, was scheduled to open on Altamont Avenue in the fall of 2014. Lofts, a grocery store and new retail enterprises also are flowing into the sector.

For Paul Karns, Tom Sullivan and Kevin O'Leary, it was a long, strange trip from the homebrewers' co-op they started in a garage on Church Hill in 2010. Sundays would find them at their half-barrel Sabco system tweaking recipes for their Saison or Honey Ginger Ale and sharing tastes with homebrewers and passersby.

Speculation about going commercial morphed into a solid business plan, but Church Hill was unfeasible for various reasons. Places in Manchester also didn't suit their needs, so Scott's Addition became a logical target. They were able to procure a zoning revision on Leigh Street, raise sufficient funds with the help of some forty investors and revitalize a former moving-and-storage building dating to 1940. Using a fifteen-barrel DME system, they began cranking out commercial versions of their yeasty-spicy Saison, the delicate Honey Ginger Ale, a wonderfully balanced and fragrant IPA and a Virginia Common ale-lager hybrid in the Anchor Steam tradition.

Ardent's building sports an attractive twenty-four-foot walnut bar, sixteen taps and a terra-cotta beer garden. The site suits not only the trio's urban instincts but also their common interest in history and developing

The second brewery to open in Richmond's Scott's Addition, Ardent Craft Ales grew from the vision of (from left) Paul Karns, Tom Sullivan and Kevin O'Leary. *Photo by Lee Graves.*

beers true to pre-Prohibition sensibilities. The brewery's name evolved from research where "ardent spirits" popped up repeatedly in references to alcohol—whether to demonize, praise or regulate it.

"What brought us together was we were all interested in the same types of beer for the same reasons," said Sullivan. "The beers we were brewing weren't beers you could readily go out and buy at the time…It made perfect sense to us to try to perfect those styles."

"At the time, there were very few saisons on the market and there were very few commons," said Karns. "A lot of the beers we were working on filled the niche we were interested in. And those just happened to be styles that were historical styles."

O'Leary, a veteran of Cambridge Brewing Company in Massachusetts and Ardent's head brewer, came on the scene after Karns and Sullivan had joined forces. "I just started hanging out, trying to contribute with my professional experience." They found kinship as homebrewers, and they don't want to forget those roots now that they've gone pro. Competitions and classes are part of their plan.

"One of the things that we're proud of is, when we were at the garage, how many people we got interested in and taught about brewing and craft beer along the way," Sullivan said. "We really want to continue to make that part of our mission."

Scott's Addition puts them in a central location in Richmond's metropolitan spread, plus it adds a pearl to the string of urban breweries lining the city's neck. "Richmond is continuing to develop into a beer town," O'Leary said. "Having more breweries is going to help everybody else. People go on 'beercations.'"

"I think people will enjoy going from place to place," Karns added. "It's a fun time to be in this market."

RUSTY BEAVER BREWERY

While Richmond and Virginia have their share of brothers in the brewing business—Phil and Chris Ray at Center of the Universe, the Shiffletts at Three Brothers Brewing in Harrisonburg—a small brewery north of RVA might be the only father-son operation. Rusty Beaver Brewery in Ladysmith grew out of the homebrewing adventures of Austin Ivey and his father, Rick. Both were enthusiastic at the outset, but as Rick puts it, "He got way more into it than I did."

A certified executive chef, Rick had built Virginia Barbeque into a thriving business with seven franchise locations. One of the sites was in a retail shopping center just off U.S. 1 in Caroline County. That store was transformed into a homebrew shop in 2012. "We had the idea right away that we would slowly turn this into a brewery," Rick said. "Part of the idea was, let's get Austin some time where he can be in here brewing."

Austin began cranking out brews on a three-barrel system, similar to the initial setup at Midnight Brewery in Goochland County. Midnight's owner, Trae Cairns, and others in Richmond's beer community (Rusty Beaver is a member of Richmond Breweries United) helped the business get started. By the first anniversary in June 2014, Austin had built a following with the likes of Roy's Big Bad Brown Ale, Buck Tooth IPA and Quake Stout.

"I think the local community has accepted us," Austin said. Demand varies according to the season, he said, but "people always dig the IPA." Nearby Timbers Restaurant has the Buck Tooth on tap, and Brown Distributing carries the brand in the Richmond area. The small brewing system limits Rusty Beaver's volume, but staying local is a priority anyway. "We're definitely the small guys in town. We're not oblivious to the fact that

Rick Ivey (left) and son Austin developed a following for Rusty Beaver Brewery with the likes of Roy's Big Bad Brown Ale, Bucktooth IPA, Quake Stout and others. *Photo by Jennifer Pullinger.*

we're thirty minutes out of Richmond and teeny," Rick said. "We don't want to have beer everywhere. We want to be small and have a niche."

Being small doesn't rule out growing. On their seventeen-acre farm about six miles away, they have planted Cascade hops and are building a facility to house a ten-barrel brewing system and tasting room. Like Lickinghole Creek Craft Brewery in Goochland County, Rusty Beaver hopes to benefit from legislation passed by the Virginia General Assembly in 2014 intended to put farm breweries on a more even footing with wineries. Officials in both Caroline and Spotsylvania Counties have been cooperative in helping the brewery succeed, Rick said.

Nina, Rick's wife and Austin's mother, pitches in by handling the bookkeeping and accounting chores, making the business more of a family affair than strictly a father-son enterprise.

ROCK BOTTOM RESTAURANT AND BREWERY

Becky Hammond doesn't like pink. But she still wears pink boots to show her solidarity with other female brewers.

Gender is generally not an issue among brewers, and women historically were the ones tending the brew pots at home. Still, the profession is largely male these days, so the Pink Boots Society has been a vital networking group for women in the business. "People just don't believe it when I tell them I brew beer," Hammond said.

She has made believers of some since shepherding the installation and startup of an eight-barrel system at the new Rock Bottom Restaurant and Brewery in Short Pump Town Center. The brewpub, which opened in June 2014, is one of more than thirty locations—and the first in six years—that have popped up since Rock Bottom opened in Denver in 1991. The brewpub showcases ten of Hammond's beers. Corporate gives guidelines—a light beer, an IPA, a red ale, a dark beer—but the recipes are hers, she said.

Hammond grew up in Nashville, Tennessee, and graduated from Clemson University with a marine science degree and an ambition to "swim with the dolphins." She discovered craft beer and got hooked on the flavor, the process and the prospects. She met Allen Corey, former CEO of the company that owns Rock Bottom, told him of her interest and was offered a spot on the brew team.

Becky Hammond, head brewer at Rock Bottom Restaurant and Brewery in Short Pump Town Center, supervised the installation of the eight-barrel system there. *Photo by Jennifer Pullinger.*

During Hammond's training in Tennessee, she worked with Brad Mortensen, a name familiar to some Richmonders. He served as head brewer of Legend Brewing Company in the 1990s. That connection has provided a link with the close-knit circle of brewers in the Richmond area, and Hammond has been active to establish herself as one of the—well, certainly not one of the guys. "This is a club. That club is my club," she said. "Gender doesn't ever factor in."

Hammond's skills were put to a tough test in June 2014. Frank Day, who founded Rock Bottom in 1991, visited the Short Pump location along with Srinivas Kumar, CEO of the parent company, CraftWorks Restaurants and Breweries, Inc. Hammond brewed a special batch of Walnut Buffalo Gold Ale for the occasion. (The name and recipe allude to the Walnut Brewery that Day and a business partner started in Boulder, Colorado, in 1990, plus the "buffalo" gives a nod to the mascot of the University of Colorado–Boulder.) The occasion spurred reminiscences of Day's first forays in the business—and he gave Hammond a solid thumbs up for the batch.

EXTRA BILLY'S SMOKEHOUSE AND BREWERY (MIDLOTHIAN)

The opening of Extra Billy's Smokehouse and Brewery on Alverser Drive in 2000 marked the first brewpub to sprout in Chesterfield County. Bill Ehlert, the first brewer, experimented with smoked beer styles to complement the restaurant's signature fare. He was succeeded in 2013 by Brandon Tolbert, an award-winning homebrewer who took the operation to a new level.

With Tolbert's move from Extra Billy's to the Answer Brewpub in 2014 (see the following section), the baton passed to Dylan Brooks, a longtime friend of Tolbert. A distinguished homebrewer in his own right, Brooks has produced a variety of beers, from barleywines to Belgian-style ales. His brewing prowess was awarded with a bronze medal for My Only Weiss at the 2014 Virginia Craft Brewers Fest.

"I like to experiment with a lot of styles, but American ales are the bread and butter," Brooks said. One priority was keeping a supply of fresh Citra Ass Down, a Tolbert creation, on tap. A single-hopped IPA made with seventeen pounds of Citra hops, Citra Ass Down earned raves for its intoxicating aroma and balanced flavor. That beer won gold at the 2013 Virginia Craft Brewers Cup competition. Brooks began establishing his own identify with

Dylan Brooks succeeded Brandon Tolbert as brewer at Extra Billy's Smokehouse and Brewery in 2014. *Photo by Lee Graves.*

a black IPA, and the Extra Billy's beer menu will include lagers as gateway beers for the non-craft crowd, as well as the hefeweizen.

Though he had never brewed professionally, Brooks said he was not naïve about the hard work involved. His background helping his father as a fisherman and crabber in Tappahannock, Virginia, was good preparation, he said. "I'm no stranger to manual labor and hard work."

Brooks's attitude and talent "will keep Extra Billy's on the beer map," said Jason Harr, who runs the family business. "Since we've stepped up our brewing of craft ales, beer enthusiasts come in for beer and enjoy our barbecue, and barbecue connoisseurs come in for barbecue and enjoy our beer. It's all good."

THE ANSWER BREWPUB

On a steamy, rain-spattered July night in Richmond, the Answer Brewpub opened its doors for the first time to kick off the 2014 Capital Ale House National Beer Expo.

An Bui checks out work on the Answer Brewpub during construction in early 2014. *Photo by Lee Graves.*

It wasn't an ideal debut—a paperwork glitch prevented the Answer from serving alcohol. That wrinkle was minor, though, as patrons shuffled between Mekong Restaurant, where copious libations were served, and the Answer, where live music and heaps of Vietnamese pub fare made for a festive occasion.

Just a few weeks earlier, An Bui, owner of both the restaurant and the brewpub, had tapped Brandon Tolbert as the Answer's brewer. "It's all about relationships. Brandon and I have a relationship," Bui said. As head brewer at Extra Billy's Smokehouse and Brewery in Midlothian, Tolbert had won awards and acclaim. He began collaborating with Bui on mighty brews such as Kong Krush, an imperial IPA made with Citra and Mosaic hops, and Good Morning Mekong, an imperial porter brewed jointly with prestigious Cigar City Brewing in Tampa, Florida.

The Answer held its official grand opening—with thirty-six taps of draft beer—in September 2014. On-site brewing, however, was not anticipated until later in the year. First, Tolbert was to oversee installation of a five-barrel direct-fire Premier system, seven five-barrel fermenters and seven bright tanks. The end goal envisioned by Bui and Tolbert was to serve the freshest of fresh beers, with the spotlight on hoppy brews. Sour and barrel-aged beverages will appear down the line. "We're just going to try to brew beers that we like to drink," Tolbert said.

The brewpub, just two doors up from Mekong on West Broad Street, occupies a sizable footprint—twelve thousand square feet across three levels with three bars, seating for five hundred and a stage for live music. The brewing equipment will be on display, as will Tolbert's talents.

A graduate of Virginia Commonwealth University's School of the Arts, Tolbert began homebrewing when his wife gave him a starter kit for Christmas one year. The effort proved a false start. "Since that first batch, I've never had to dump a batch of beer," Tolbert said. He went on to become a prominent member of James River Homebrewers and sponsor a homebrewing competition at Extra Billy's. Winning medals and praise for his beers signaled his status as a rising star; moving to the Answer cemented his standing. "It's a huge step for me," Tolbert said when the announcement was made. "I couldn't have asked for anything better."

RICHMOND BREWERIES UNITED

In August 2014, brewers and brewery owners joined forces to launch Richmond Breweries United. The nonprofit coalition, a partnership with Richmond Region Tourism, "was formed to advocate Richmond beer culture and Richmond tourism," said Jacob Brunow, craft and import director for Brown Distributing Company.

A key element is the Richmond Beer Trail, a map giving locations, backgrounds and contact information for RVA breweries, as well as a list of restaurants and stores that feature local craft beer. The map is available in hard copy at area breweries, and additional details are online at www.rvabeer.com.

BREWERIES IN PLANNING

Garden Grove Brewing Company

After originally seeking a site in Chesterfield County, Garden Grove Brewing Company planted its roots in the western end of Carytown in 2014. That summer, construction was underway on a 1,600-square-foot tasting room with a theme that will combine a modern look with a nod to West Cary Street's colorful past.

"We're thinking of having a speakeasy theme," said brewmaster Mike Brandt. Rich, dark colors; barrels for patrons to sit or stand at; couches; and coffee tables were envisioned as elements of the décor. "We want something that really pops."

Brandt said he and partners Ryan Mitchell and Mike Davis were anticipating opening in early November 2014 using a three-barrel system with four fermentation tanks and two bright tanks. British and Belgian styles will dominate the offerings, with the latter making use of Brandt's background in winemaking as well as brewing. "Yeast flavors are the number one thing for me. You have to have the malt to back it up, then hops and spices," Brandt said. Expect a Belgian dubbel, with strong plum and chocolate notes, and a saison using hibiscus, rose hips and dried fruits.

Second to yeast in his priorities will be using raisins, beginning in the boil. Brandt also will use a "solera" aging system similar to that in the wine industry for brews such as his imperial stout. (The method entails adding younger beer to varying levels of more mature beer in barrels to achieve a complex blending process.)

The site has a total of 3,700 square feet, including an upstairs level that could be used for a pool table, darts and other amusements. The brewery has two restaurants for neighbors—Nacho Mama's and Philly Steak & Gyros—and Brandt said both are excited to be playing off the brewery's offerings. "This is supposed to be fun for all of us," he said.

Stone Brewing Company

As this book was going to press, RVA's beer community was holding its collective breath at the prospect of California-based Stone Brewing Company building a regional facility in Richmond. Stone announced in early August

2014 that Richmond was on the short list, along with Columbus, Ohio, and Norfolk, Virginia.

The brewery foresees an investment of $47 million over the first five years. Operations would be housed in a facility of at least 130,000 square feet (with the potential to expand) and employ up to 103 people. Stone wants to brew 120,000 barrels a year with the possibility of increasing to 500,000 barrels (a barrel equals thirty-one gallons). A restaurant and retail stores also are planned.

Known for its Arrogant Bastard ale and other aggressive, innovative brews, Stone Brewing Company is one of San Diego's key businesses. The brewery was founded in 1996 by Greg Koch and Steve Wagner and had grown to become the tenth-largest craft brewery in the United States by 2013, with plans to open a brewing facility in Berlin.

One potential site for Stone in Richmond—twelve and a half acres of mostly publically owned land east of downtown—presents an interesting historic coincidence. The nearby Fulton Hill area is where Powhatans were living when Captain John Smith and Christopher Newport arrived from Jamestown in 1607 bearing wine, brandy and—as you might recall from Chapter 1—"beere."

7 Hills Brewing Company

For years, Richmonders had heard about the possibility of Haxall Brewing Company opening a downtown brewpub. That has morphed into 7 Hills Brewing Company, which is predicting a fall 2014 opening in Shockoe Bottom.

Head brewer Jeff Metz will be developing recipes inspired by the James River, including Texas Beach ThaiPA. I remember drinking it when the Beeristoric Tour made its stop by the Yuengling caves at Rocketts Landing some years ago. Also on the beer menu will be 7 Hills Saison, Pipeline Pale Ale and Belle Isle Blonde.

Black Heath Meadery

Adding to the imbibing options in Scott's Addition, Black Heath Meadery was on course to open in late 2014 with an array of options for this ancient beverage. Owner Bill Cavender, who has been making mead since 1991, anticipated initially offering traditional mead (just honey), ginger mead, raspberry mead and a surprise entry.

Technically, mead falls under regulations governing a commercial winery, which will allow Black Heath to self-distribute. Given the location near Ardent Craft Ales, Isley Brewing Company—both in Scott's Addition—and Hardywood Park Craft Brewery on the east side of the Boulevard, RVA's craft beer scene figures to give the meadery a bump in exposure.

"Craft beer opened people's palates up," Cavender told beer writer Annie Tobey in a Richmond.com article. "People in Richmond are discerning, but they're willing to experiment and try new stuff."

9

LOOKING AROUND THE STATE

The growth evident in Richmond's beer scene has been mirrored around the state—a reflection of the cultural shift that has spurred the blossoming of beer culture throughout the nation.

Consider this: In 2011, before Senate Bill 604 became law, Virginia had 44 active breweries. By 2014, the number had risen to more than 85, with hopes of growing to 150 in the next three to five years. Breweries have sprung up in every corner of the state: O'Connor, Smartmouth and Young Veterans to the east; Adroit Theory, Lost Rhino and Port City to the north; Sunken City, Parkway and Wolf Hills to the southwest; Three Brothers, Redbeard and Pale Fire in the Shenandoah Valley; and Three Notch'd, Wild Wolf and Blue Mountain in the shadow of the Blue Ridge.

"The pace at which the number of breweries is opening is something I would not have suspected," said Mark Thompson, co-founder of Starr Hill Brewery and the 2014 chair of the Virginia Craft Brewers Guild, an affiliate of the Virginia Manufacturers Association.

SETTING A STANDARD OF EXCELLENCE

It's not just numbers. State breweries have won some of the most prestigious awards possible. Devils Backbone Brewing Company's Basecamp in Nelson County was named Small Brewing Company and Small Brewpub of the

Right: Few breweries have a manifesto, but Adroit Theory in Loudoun County's Purcellville is not your mainstream operation. *Photo by Lee Graves.*

Below: Mark Thompson, 2014 chairman of the Virginia Craft Brewers Guild, has led Starr Hill to prominence as a regional brewery. *Photo by Lee Graves.*

Year in 2013 and 2012, respectively, at the Great American Beer Festival in Denver. Devils Backbone head brewer Jason Oliver won top individual honors in those categories as well.

The state sparkles with medals. Starr Hill added to its collection with a gold in the 2014 World Beer Cup for its Whiter Shade of Pale Ale. Smartmouth brought home bronze from the 2013 GABF for its Notch 9 Double IPA. In fact, Virginia ranked fourth among all states in the number of medals won at the 2013 GABF.

Breweries have become destinations that feed $21.2 billion in economic impact through tourism. They are part of a broader context that includes food and other alcoholic beverages—wine, cider, whiskey. "We see the entire culinary environment as one that's extremely attractive to travelers," said Rita McClenny, president and CEO of the Virginia Tourism Corporation. "People are looking for unique experiences. When they go to a destination, they can come home with a fantastic story of 'I had this, I did this.'"

Tourism dollars are only one slice of the pie. The total comes to $623 million and 8,163 jobs in terms of economic impact from craft brewing, according to the manufacturers' association. Include the major players, MillerCoors in the Shenandoah Valley and Anheuser-Busch in Williamsburg, and you can add millions more. And there are support businesses—canning and bottling operations, for example.

LOVE ON TAP

In 2012, the Virginia General Assembly designated August as Virginia Craft Beer Month—"Love on Tap," as the marketing slogan says. That observance reaches its climax at the Virginia Craft Brewers Fest, which includes a competitive angle: the Virginia Craft Brewers Cup. Devils Backbone won the Best of Show gold award three years running and in 2014 swept the category.

Not only is Devils Backbone setting a high standard for the quality of its beers, but the brewery also forged ahead of Starr Hill as the state's leader in volume in 2014, thanks to its "Outpost" facility near Lexington. Working with economic development folks in Rockbridge County, Steve Crandall, the brewery's founder, and others developed plans for a fifteen-thousand-square-foot facility on twelve acres owned by the county. Construction of the first phase began in the spring of 2011 with expectations of creating ten jobs in three years and producing thirty thousand barrels in ten years. Instead, more than three dozen jobs opened, two more construction phases have been completed and the brewery forecast forty thousand to fifty thousand barrels in 2014.

At the eastern end of the state, another construction project was underway in 2014. Green Flash Brewing Company of San Diego was erecting a fifty-eight-thousand-square-foot facility in Virginia Beach expected to employ more than forty people. Plans are to open in 2015 and ultimately reach a production capacity of 100,000 barrels a year. A beer garden for imbibers and a yeast lab available to other brewers are part of the scenario.

"A Great Place to Do Business"

"Virginia is a great place to do business, has a developing craft beer culture and Virginia Beach felt like home," Lisa Hinkley, Green Flash co-founder, said in announcing the expansion location.

Betsy O'Brien manages the Harrisonburg taproom that Three Notch'd Brewing Company of Charlottesville opened in 2014. *Photo by Lee Graves.*

Green Flash is, of course, known for its West Coast–style IPAs—Palate Wrecker, Green Bullet, Road Warrior and the signature West Coast IPA. And while Virginia brewers have also shown a knack for IPAs (witness Smartmouth's Notch 9), it is the diversity of beers brewed in the state that is perhaps its greatest distinction. Pick a style—saison, kölsch, gose, altbier, rauchbier, barleywine, stout, imperial stout, oyster stout, porter, bock, maibock, eisbock, Oktoberfest, sours, barrel-aged whatevers—and you can find brews that adhere to stylistic standard, as well as brews that are totally, wonderfully off any chart. At least one brewery, Lost Rhino, has even put out a brew using all-Virginia ingredients.

Which brings us to the tangents of the brewing scene. Hop production has spread some tender shoots through groups such as the Old Dominion Hops Co-op and the Virginia Hop Initiative, as well as businesses such as Huguenot Hops and Piedmont Hops (see Chapter 11). Growers also are experimenting with barley, with help from researchers at several universities.

Combine all those ingredients and you understand why the state crackles with optimism when it comes to the craft beer scene. "Virginia is getting on the map," said Bill Butcher, founder of Port City Brewing Company in Alexandria. "It's developing a reputation nationally for great beer."

10

LOOKING INTO A CRYSTAL BALL

In May 2014, three folks from the Brewers Association—aka Craft Beer Central—visited Richmond. They sampled local beers, visited the Yuengling caves and other sites and conducted a look at Virginia's future for a roomful of brewery owners, brewers and state and local officials.

Julia Herz, craft beer program director for the association, rattled off statistics and buzzed through PowerPoint graphics outlining key statistics: 52 percent annual growth in volume among Virginia craft breweries compared with 18 percent nationally; a ranking of fifteenth in the nation in 2013 for the number of active breweries in the state with 61 (in June 2014, there were more than 85); and the possibility to grow to 150 breweries in the next three to five years.

"I feel you guys are making a play to be on the map of meccas for beer. That is a huge, fantastic and possible goal," Herz said. "Part of what I want to do is to applaud you guys and encourage you to be on that map."

Looking into the future requires understanding the present. Market share plays into the equation. Nationwide, craft beer in early 2014 commanded 7.8 percent market share by volume (15.3 million barrels) and 14.3 percent by sales ($14.3 billion), according to the Brewers Association. Virginia craft beers represented 2 percent of all the beers sold in the state. By comparison, Oregon's beers occupy an 18 percent share of the state's market; in Portland, that figure hangs around 30 percent and can spike seasonally to 50 percent.

So the numbers say there's room to grow; the craft sector has been increasing production by double digits for several years. But that growth

Julia Herz, craft beer program director for the Brewers Association based in Colorado, chats with Strangeways owner Neil Burton during a 2014 visit. *Photo by Lee Graves.*

comes at the expense of mainstream brewers when you look at the overall industry trend—down 1.9 percent in 2013 and flat at best over the last few years. Let us not forget that Bud Light and Miller Lite are the top-selling beers in the country and that Anheuser-Busch and MillerCoors have production facilities in the state.

Growth depends on a nurturing environment. The passage of significant legislation by the General Assembly bodes well; Senate Bill 604 changed the landscape by allowing retail sales at breweries, and Senate Bill 430 intended to create a more level playing field among wineries and farm breweries.

More than forty breweries, including Flying Mouse of Botetourt County, poured beers at the 2014 Big Lick Beertopia in Salem. *Photo by Lee Graves.*

Localities are realizing that small breweries can be good members of the community—family-oriented destinations that attract tourists, provide jobs, support local charities and pay taxes. Festivals draw thousands, and even the release of special beers has proved a magnet. Adam Shifflett of Three Brothers Brewing Company in Harrisonburg said folks from eight states came for the release of its Resolute Bourbon Barrel Imperial Stout.

In her talk, Herz described the movement underway as a cultural shift, part of a broader food arts movement. Part of the lesson of this book is that, in addition to the shift, the current direction can be viewed as a cultural correction. As we have seen, in the late 1800s, the country had thousands of breweries. Prohibition, grain shortages in the Depression, grain rationing in World War II and consolidation among breweries caused its own cultural shift.

I'll leave it to Eric McKay, co-founder of Hardywood Park Craft Brewery, to voice the final words. At the same roundtable that Herz attended, McKay said the state's potential was a fundamental reason for choosing Richmond as a location.

"At the time, Virginia was thirty-seventh in the country in terms of breweries per capita. We felt like there was really nothing that would be preventing us from becoming a top-ten state in breweries per capita and to have a phenomenal craft beer scene," McKay said. "I hope it's not long before anyone in the world hears the word 'Virginia' and immediately thinks of great beer."

11

BEYOND THE BREW HOUSE

Some have helped create Richmond's thriving brewing culture. Others are sustaining it. And still others are exploring new ways to support and supply it. Here's a look.

MEKONG RESTAURANT

This is where Richmonders come for answers about beer. What's the latest? What's the freshest? What's the barrel-aged-est? What's the sourest?

An Bui has the answers. Actually, Bui has only one answer. "Beer is the answer. That is the gospel I always preach on," says Bui, chief beer officer. "And I believe it."

The gospel according to Mekong has led the restaurant to three consecutive first-place awards in craftbeer.com's Great American Beer Bars contest. In February 2014, *Draft* magazine listed Virginia as one of "four states to beer-tour now," mentioning Mekong and "its 50 constantly rotating taps [as] the undisputed hub for tasting stellar pours." When brothers Todd and Jason Alström of *BeerAdvocate* magazine came to Richmond for a brew tour that month, they hop-scotched from Hardywood to Isley to Strangeways and then ended at Mekong, where a crowd bumped elbows and raised glasses in a show of Richmond love. Their impression? "World-class, 99 out of 100," they posted on the *BeerAdvocate* website.

Jerome Rebetez (right) of Brasserie des Franches-Montagnes in Switzerland visits with fans at Mekong Restaurant in Richmond. *Photo by Lee Graves.*

Don't expect swollen heads when you go, though. Bui routinely greets regulars personally, often with something new to taste. The young men behind the bar are generous with samples. Handwritten (scrawled?) notes cover several boards describing what's on the fifty taps. Nothing fancy. "We try to make this place feel like home; it has a heart," Bui says. "We try to be local, try to provide the best beer we can for the local [customers]. And the local is who make this place happen."

It's sort of an odd development for Bui and his family, who fled Vietnam when he was ten. They landed in Richmond and in 1995 bought an existing restaurant at Mekong's current location on West Broad Street. Bui became manager and began introducing Belgian beers because they paired well with the Vietnamese cuisine, the bottles were elegant, the beer was delicious and everybody else in town was doing the wine thing.

Belgians still pepper the list, as do rarities from the Bruery, Firestone Walker, Cigar City, Goose Island, Victory and other U.S. breweries. But what really rock the selection are the local beers—sour from Strangeways, tripel from Lickinghole Creek, gingerbread stout from Hardywood, IPA from Extra Billy's.

CAPITAL ALE HOUSE

The heart of Richmond pumps around Capital Ale House's downtown location with a unique urban beat. Vehicles clatter one way west on Main Street. Pedestrians—some shuffling disheveled, others banker bustling—stream along the sidewalks. The engine of economy hums in the capital's tallest buildings, and if you cock your ear the right way, you can hear the Old Richmond drawling accents mixed with the "Yo! Sup?" of the hip and now.

Go through the narrow wooden doors and inside the medley continues. A long, old-school wooden bar with a cutting-edge ice slick to keep the glasses chilled. Downstairs, darts and pool in the pub. In the music hall, homegrown blues and art school edge.

And on tap? You name it. Fifty-plus of locals like Legend, Virginia blue ribbons like Devils Backbone, national names like Dogfish Head, imports like Hacker-Pschorr and, yes, lights and lites and whatever else hits the spot. "Our distinction is that we have something for everybody here," says Matthew Simmons, president and co-founder. "In terms of staff and what we offer, we can appeal to everybody—the beer neophyte as well as the hardcore enthusiast."

The building dates to 1895. The beer dates to the freshest Simmons can get, and that means RVA and VA foremost. "We've made a very big commitment to Richmond and Virginia beers," Simmons says. "We devote more than one hundred taps to them, company-wide. I'm proud to say we pour more Virginia beers than anyone."

The company includes four additional locations. Two are in Greater Richmond—Innsbrook and Midlothian—with others in Fredericksburg and Harrisonburg. Simmons wants to arm wrestle anyone who suggests that more than one restaurant/pub evokes the word "chain." "When we started, I don't think we even thought about multiple locations," he says.

Actually, Simmons fled the corporate chain environment after nine years with Applebee's when he landed a job as general manager of Legend's pub in 1997. Five years there convinced him and three others—Chris Holder and Mike and Linda Jones—of Richmond's capacity to grow great beer and serve a beer-loving community. In 2014, the business had 371 taps and more than three hundred employees and provided a meeting place not only for chatting imbibers but also for movers and shakers—women discussing their role in the industry, brewers and legislators planning for the Virginia Beer Caucus, history geeks gathering for the annual Beeristoric Tour. In July 2014, Capital Ale House was the name sponsor of the inaugural National Beer Expo in Richmond; the following month, it hosted the debut of *From Grain to Growler,* a documentary about craft beer in Virginia.

COMMERCIAL TAPHOUSE & GRILL

"The search for a perfect pint should last a lifetime." You'll find those words—the motto of the late, great beer writer Michael Jackson—on the back of Commercial Taphouse & Grill T-shirts. For co-founder James Talley, the words might as well be carved on his heart.

Talley and friend Jim Dickerson combined their backgrounds—Talley on the restaurant side, Dickerson as a homebrewer—in the early 1990s to follow their passion for craft beer and food by opening Commercial Taphouse & Grill on Robinson Street in the Fan District. To put this in perspective, Legend and Richbrau were at the time pioneering the brewing side of the craft beer movement in Manchester and Shockoe Slip, respectively.

Talley had gone to New York with dreams of being a musician, gotten a job at the Hard Rock Café there and then moved to another Hard Rock in northern Virginia. That's where his beer candle got lit. "I had been drinking imports. I went into a store and picked up a six-pack of Old Dominion ale. To me, it was pretty much life-changing," he said.

Dickerson and Talley began doing beer dinners at another restaurant and then brought their passion for beer to Commercial Taphouse. From the outset, the beer list was daring. Bottles of Belgian heavy hitters were on one side of the original menu; on the other were taps of Anchor Steam, Stoudt's Maibock, Wild Goose and a brew with a local connection—Nickel Bridge Lager. An early highlight was tapping the first keg of Legend Brown Ale in 1994. "That was like the next life-changing thing," Talley said.

Over the years, Commercial Taphouse has become a local institution. Dimly lit, festooned with Christmas tree lights and memorabilia, a beer engine for cask-conditioned brews, bands occasionally squeezed against a back wall—it has thrived by being endearingly quirky. The two founders opened another taphouse in Norfolk and a short-lived brewpub in Virginia Beach. Eventually, Dickerson bowed out of the business; Talley continued as president.

In July 2014, another life-changing event occurred when Talley announced the sale of the Taphouse to An Bui, magnate of Mekong Restaurant and the Answer Brewpub (see earlier sections). Bui pledged to retain the flavor of the establishment, though alterations in draft beer service and cuisine were planned. Bui also said Sean O'Hern, a fixture at the Taphouse and its cousin, the Cask Café, would continue in a key position. "To me, James is the godfather of the craft beer scene in town," Bui said. "He was the one to build the first taphouse in town. For us, for me, to take over from James, it's actually an honor."

For Talley, it was an ideal transition. "To know An is coming in here, what I said was 'He's the person for the next twenty years.'"

As for the past two decades, Talley reflected on his legacy. "If I'm known for anything in Richmond, it's because we brought craft beer—local beer—here and to Norfolk," Talley said. "That's not a small thing. It's really a pretty big thing."

BEER DISTRIBUTORS

The RVA metro area is served by three major beer wholesalers: Brown Distributing Company, Loveland Distributing Company and Specialty Beverage of Virginia.

A family-owned operation serving parts of Virginia and Florida, Brown distributes Budweiser, Bud Light and other Anheuser-Busch products. The company initiated a "Taste the Local" concept at its Richmond site several years ago after employees visited craft beer meccas around the country and saw connections among local breweries, local businesses and local food. As of mid-2014, Brown's craft department was distributing beer from all of Richmond's local breweries.

As noted earlier, Loveland Distributing Company was founded in 1953 and purchased by Leon Stepanian Sr. in 1958. MillerCoors products dominate domestic offerings, with Corona and Guinness leading the imports. Among craft beers, Loveland carries Samuel Adams and has introduced several craft brands in RVA, including Boulevard and Sweetwater breweries. In addition, it has worked with Wild Wolf Brewing Company in Nellysford, Virginia, to develop specialty brews for the Richmond Folk Festival and the Richmond Kickers soccer team.

Founded in 1991 by Bobby Roberts, Specialty Beverage of Virginia was acquired by L. Knife & Son, Inc. in 2009 and then by Reed's Incorporated in 2010. In addition to celebrated Belgian beers such as Chimay and Duvel, the distributor carries nationally known craft brands such as Dogfish Head, Firestone Walker, Stone and Green Flash. Its portfolio also includes Virginia's Blue Mountain, Parkway and Beach breweries.

OLD DOMINION MOBILE CANNING

The city that made history with the first beer in cans is providing opportunities for another canning enterprise. Mike Horn, a resident of Glen Allen, started Old Dominion Mobile Canning in April 2013, and roughly a year later, he put the lid on his millionth can of craft beer. In addition, the spring of 2014 saw him planning to expand to a second canning line.

A homebrewer for years, Horn initially dreamed about starting his own brewery. When Hardywood Park Craft Brewery opened in 2011, however, "they set the bar so high" that he recalibrated his vision.

What caught his eye was the success of Colorado's Oskar Blues Brewery, which pioneered craft beer in cans in 2002. Horn invested just under $250,000

Cans of Hardywood Park's Great Return IPA are filled by Old Dominion Mobile Canning during a session at the brewery. *Photo by Lee Graves.*

in a system from a neighbor of Oskar Blues—Mobile Canning Systems in Longmont, Colorado. Old Dominion was the first mobile canning operation east of the Mississippi River and the fourth in the country.

Now, canned craft beer is no longer a novelty. In early 2014, more than four hundred craft breweries in all fifty states were canning 1,462 beers in ninety-three different styles, according to craftcans.com.

GROWING HOPS

Eat local, drink local—and grow local.

That could easily be the motto for craft beer lovers who have their fingers in the dirt, especially those with green thumbs for hops. "There really is a true potential for Virginia brewers to tap into the growing support for the local food movement throughout Virginia," said Jonathan Scott of the Virginia Hop Initiative.

Commercially, the Richmond area has proved fertile for Huguenot Hops and Piedmont Hops, which also has a location in North Carolina. Both businesses are members of the Old Dominion Hops Co-Op, headed by Stan Driver. Pardon the pun, but he was a driving force in getting hops growing in Virginia through his Hoot'n Holler Hops business and with Blue Mountain Brewery in Nelson County.

I've been told, though I have yet to see a primary source on this, that Virginia once was the second leading hops producer in the country. Thomas Jefferson grew hops for brewing at Monticello, and Martha, his wife, purchased them as well from local slaves.

Its reemergence is in its infancy. Growers in Washington State harvested 27,062 acres of hops in 2013, according to the U.S. Department of Agriculture. Virginia had about 30 acres in hops in 2014, Driver said. Cascade is the dominant variety. "Cascade is the most resilient in our area for all farmers," said Devon Kistler of Huguenot Hops. "It's easier to grow with our temperature, humidity and daylight hours."

The zeal for hops' zing is nurtured by Hardywood Park Craft Brewery through its Community Hopping Project. The brewery supplies rhizomes to growers, mostly hobbyists. In return, they share some of their yield, which Hardywood uses for its RVA IPA.

Piedmont also has given and sold hops to spur the spread. "Everybody that we've given hops to or even sold hops to has thoroughly enjoyed our

Kurt Stanfield (left) and Devon Kistler monitor the growth of Cascade bines at their Huguenot Hops farm in Chesterfield County. *Photo by Lee Graves.*

product, so that's good," said David Goode in the documentary *From Grain to Growler*. Goode, who runs the business along with Steve Brown, said they had about 250 plants in their Chesterfield County operation in 2014.

Huguenot Hops has about 3.0 acres dedicated to hops with about 1.25 acres actively growing, Kistler said. The plots are carved out of 12.0 acres already owned by Kurt Stanfield, Kistler's business partner. Though he's an accountant by profession, Stanfield has farming in his blood—his grandparents owned a farm in Dinwiddie County. He was ready for an agricultural venture when Kistler, a homebrewer, pitched the idea. In 2014, their second year as a commercial operation, they expected to gather five to six hundred pounds from 1,200 plants of three hop varieties—Cascade, Nugget and Zeus.

Scott's group supplied Virginia Willamette for Buncha Crazies Double IPA, brewed for the grand opening of the Three Notch'd Brewing Company taproom in Harrisonburg. "That was actually the first time we have ever used local hops in a brew, but we plan on doing it more," said brewmaster Dave Warwick.

While brewers want to be supportive of the local product, quality and price are business considerations. Hops straight from the bines, or "wet hops," must be used quickly—a good thing in capturing flavor and aroma for special brews. But for year-round flagship beers, pellet hops purchased in bulk from established producers with analysis of acids and oils go a long way to ensure consistency and control costs. Warwick said he is happy to pay extra for local hops but would probably have to pass the cost along to customers. "We're finding in Charlottesville and in Harrisonburg that folks have no problem shelling out an extra buck or two to support local," he said.

Yeast Specialists

Jason Ridlon and Malachy McKenna, both homebrewers, combined their backgrounds in microbiology and chemical ecology to start RVA Yeast Labs in December 2013. Their specialty is isolating local yeast strains, but their business offers a range of yeasts, including Brettanomyces, as well as lactobacillus and pediococcus bacterial strains.

Ridlon and McKenna have worked with Lickinghole Creek Craft Brewery and Black Heath Meadery to produce unique batches in the commercial realm. Their yeasts also are carried by Original Gravity and WeekEnd Brewer homebrewing supply stores. Check out their website at www.rvayeastlabs.com.

Breweriana

The Richbrau Chapter of the Brewery Collectibles Club of America has been, as its newsletter says, "serving the lunatic fringe since 1978." Members collect cans, bottles and many other items associated with beer and brewing, particularly those associated with Home Brewing Company and Richbrau Brewing Company. The club helps put on breweriana events, including the Monticello Extravaganza Beer Can & Breweriana Show and a local event each year. The club's website is www.richbrauchapter.com.

The Richmond Area Bottle Collectors Association, formed in 1970, goes far beyond beer in its collectibles, but the brews of yesteryear are definitely included in the interests of members. The group's website is http://home.comcast.net/~edandlucy1/RABCA.html.

Staying Connected

Just as Richmond has a bounty of breweries to keep aficionados on their toes, beer lovers have a bevy of groups to help them stay in the know. Here are some I've found helpful in getting the most out of a great thing.

Trinkin.com

In 2013, four Richmonders put their heads together to create a mobile website to pair seekers of good beers with places to enjoy them. "We were talking about various ways to spotlight what's going on in Richmond," said Andy Frank, one of Trinkin's founders.

More than sixty area restaurants, bars, taphouses and breweries are Trinkin "buddies," as Frank calls them. They provide regular updates on the beers, ciders, cocktails and other beverages available at their establishments. And if you choose not to drive after imbibing, Trinkin provides links to taxicab services. In 2014, Trinkin expanded into the Charlottesville and Harrisonburg areas.

Richmond Beer Lovers

In May 2010, Amy Kramer met a friend on the patio of Capital Ale House in Innsbrook. An avid beer lover, Kramer had been running a Meetup group devoted to the theater and movies.

"I mentioned that I'd been thinking about starting a beer Meetup group," Kramer said. "I knew we had several friends that would definitely join, and I figured that would be a start." Response was immediate—another beer lover who overheard their conversation chimed in, "I'm in!"

The group now has more than one thousand members and has hosted more than one hundred events.

River City Beer Betties

Another group with a strong Facebook presence, the Beer Betties evolved from a group of friends who shared a certain attitude toward beer. "We were all of the 'don't push a light beer my way because I'm a woman' mind-

Amy Kramer (center) meets with legions of the Richmond Beer Lovers Meetup group at Isley Brewing Company. *Photo by Lee Graves.*

set," said founding member Hilary Langford. On a trip to Asheville, North Carolina, she saw a flier for the Asheville Beer Divas. "That sparked the bigger idea to rally all beer-loving ladies of RVA."

The Beer Betties have helped organize forums and hosted local events such as the Cards Against Humanity throw down at Strangeways Brewing. And supportive dudes are welcome as well.

RVA Rural Beer Brigade

Originally organized by Powhatan County resident Jeremy Joyce to bring together craft beer lovers living in outlying communities, the Brigade is not just for ruralists. Connecting with the larger scene, in Richmond and beyond, is part of the mission, Joyce said. "With the opening of Lickinghole Creek [in 2013] and the expansion of Midnight [in 2014], there is more traffic coming to the rural areas in search of good beer." The Brigade, started in March 2013, has more than one hundred members.

Here are more groups and sites on the Web, Facebook and Twitter (closed groups on Facebook require approval to join—just ask):

RVA Beermeister

Richmond's Beermeister, Sterling Stokes Jr., provides a steady stream of reliable information about "great beer, great food and everything in between."

Richmond Beer Elite (Closed)

With more than two thousand members, the Beer Elite serves as one of RVA's essential forums for comparing notes on beers and breweries, posting events and discussing industry trends.

Fans of Virginia Craft Breweries (Open)

The name says it all for this group, which has more than 1,240 members.

RVA Beer Tastes & Trades (Closed)

Looking for a particular beer? Want to trade? Ask to join the three-hundred-plus enthusiasts here.

Richmond Beer Experience (Closed)

The 174 members post events and ask, "Are you [beer] experienced?"

RVA Homebrewers (Open)

More than eighty members post tips and suggestions about homebrewing.

Virginia Beer Trail

A good source for maps, events, news and reviews.

VACraftBeer.com

Another handy website for what's going on in the state's craft beer community.

Links

Trinkin.com, www.trinkin.com
Richmond Beer Lovers, www.facebook.com/RVABeerLovers
River City Beer Betties, www.rvabeerbetties.com
RVA Rural Beer Brigade, www.facebook.com/groups/230123470465361
RVABeermeister, www.RVABeermeister.com
Richmond Beer Elite, www.facebook.com/groups/richmond.beer.elite
Fans of Virginia Craft Breweries, www.facebook.com/groups/347348308708958
RVA Beer Tastes & Trades, www.facebook.com/groups/rvatastesandtrades
Richmond Beer Experience, www.facebook.com/groups/444851902294303
RVA Homebrewers, www.facebook.com/groups/649894978366924
Virginia Beer Trail, www.vabeertrail.net
VACraftBeer.com, www.vacraftbeer.com

APPENDIX

RICHMOND-AREA BREWERIES, BREWPUBS

(Unless noted as having a restaurant, most breweries have tasting rooms, food trucks, outdoor seating and regular live music.)

Answer Brewpub
6008 West Broad Street, Richmond, VA
(804) 282-1248
www.theanswerbrewpub.com
@TheAnswerBrewpub
Restaurant, thirty-six taps, brewing on-site expected late 2014

Ardent Craft Ales
3200 West Leigh Street, Richmond, VA
(804) 359-1605
www.ardentcraftales.com
@ArdentCraftAles

Center of the Universe Brewing Company
11293 Air Park Road, Ashland, VA 23005
(804) 368-0299
www.cotubrewing.com
@COTUbrew

APPENDIX

Extra Billy's Smokehouse and Brewery, Midlothian location
1110 Alverser Drive, Midlothian, VA 23113
(804) 379-8727
www.extrabillys.com
Restaurant, bar

Hardywood Park Craft Brewery
2408 Ownby Lane, Richmond, VA 23220
(804) 420-2420
www.hardywood.com
@Hardywood
Multiple tasting rooms

Isley Brewing Company
1715 Summit Avenue, Richmond, VA 23230
(804) 499-0721
www.isleybrewingcompany.com
@isleybrewing

Legend Brewing Company
321 West Seventh Street, Richmond, VA 23224
(804) 232-3446
www.legendbrewing.com
@LegendBrewingCo
Restaurant, bar

Lickinghole Creek Craft Brewery
4100 Knolls Point Road, Goochland, VA 23063
(804) 314-4380
www.lickingholecreek.com
@LCCB_FarmBrews
Farmland setting

Midnight Brewery
2410 Granite Ridge Road #5, Rockville, VA 23146
(804) 356-9379
www.midnight-brewery.com
@midnightbrewery
Multiple tasting rooms

Rock Bottom Restaurant and Brewery
Short Pump Town Center
11800 West Broad Street, Richmond, VA 23233
(804) 237-1684
www.rockbottom.com
@RockBottomRVA
Restaurant, bar

Rusty Beaver Brewery
18043 Jefferson Davis Highway, Ruther Glen, VA 22546
(540) 220-8100
www.rustybeaverbrewery.com
@RustyBeaverBrew

Strangeways Brewing
2277A Dabney Road, Richmond, VA 23230
(804) 303-4336
www.strangewaysbrewing.com
@StrangewaysRVA
Multiple tasting rooms

Triple Crossing Brewing Company
113 South Foushee Street, Richmond, VA 23220
(804) 314-9219
www.triplecrossingbeer.com
@TripleCrossing

RICHMOND-AREA RESTAURANTS, TAPHOUSES

This is a partial list of destinations that have significant selections of craft beer. Unless otherwise noted, most also offer bottled beer, wine, cider, food and spirits.

American Tap Room
1601 Willow Lawn Drive, #840, Richmond, VA 23230
(804) 308-9013
www.americantaproom.com
@ATRRVA
Thirty-six beer taps, one cask

Brew Gastro Pub
6525 Centralia Road, Chesterfield, VA 23832
(804) 454-0605
www.brewgastropub.com
Thirty beer taps
Also: 11400 West Huguenot Road, Midlothian, VA 23113
Seventy beer taps

The Bucket Trade
River's Bend Boulevard, Chester, VA 23836
(804) 322-3372
www.thebuckettrade.com
@TheBucketTrade
Fourteen beer taps

Capital Ale House
Three Richmond area locations (also in Harrisonburg and Fredericksburg)
Downtown, 623 East Main Street, Richmond, VA 23219
Innsbrook, 4024-A Cox Road, Glen Allen, VA 23060
Midlothian, 13831 Village Place Drive, Midlothian, VA 23114
(804) 780-ALES
www.capitalalehouse.com
@CapitalAleHouse
More than 370 taps (all locations)
The Downtown Music Hall has regular live music

The Cask Café & Market
206 South Robinson Street, Richmond, VA 23220
(804) 355-2402
www.thecaskrva.com
@TheCaskCafe
Twelve beer taps

Commercial Taphouse & Grill
111 North Robinson Street, Richmond, VA 23220
(804) 359-6544
Facebook: www.facebook.com/pages/Commercial-Taphouse-Grill/98173184766
Fifteen beer taps, beer engine

APPENDIX

Fat Dragon
1200 North Boulevard, Richmond, VA 23230
(804) 354-9888
www.fatdragonrva.com
@FatDragonRVA
Twenty-three beer taps

Hurley's Tavern
4028-J Cox Road, Glen Allen, VA 23060
(804) 433-3332
www.hurleystavern.com
@hurleystavern
Sixteen beer taps

Joe's Inn
205 North Shields Avenue, Richmond, VA 23220
(804) 355-2282
www.joesinnrva.com
Twenty-four beer taps

Mekong Restaurant
6004 West Broad Street, Henrico, VA 23230
(804) 288-8929
www.mekongisforbeerlovers.com
@MekongRVa
Fifty-two beer taps

Mellow Mushroom
3012 West Cary Street, Richmond, VA 23221
(804) 370-8210
www.mellowmushroom.com
@MMCarytown
Thirty-nine beer taps

O'Toole's Restaurant & Pub
4800 Forest Hill Avenue, Richmond, VA 23225
(804) 233-1781
www.otoolesrestaurant.com
@OToolesPub
Richmond's oldest Irish pub

APPENDIX

Penny Lane Pub
421 East Franklin Street, Richmond, VA 23219
(804) 780-1682
www.pennylanepub.com
@PennyLanePubRVA
Traditional English pub with darts, pool and tons of Beatles memorabilia

The Pig & Pearl
2053 West Broad Street, Richmond, VA 23220
(804) 447-2016
www.thepigandpearl.com
@thepigandpearl
Twenty beer taps, with BURN, a high-end cigar and spirits lounge

Portrait House
2907 West Cary Street, Richmond, VA 23221
(804) 278-9800
www.portrait-house.com
@portrait_house
More than twenty beer taps

Rare Olde Times Public House
10602 Patterson Avenue, Richmond, VA 23238
(804) 750-1346
www.rareoldetimes.com
@RareOldePub
Irish pub with thirteen beer taps

Saison
23 West Marshall Street, Richmond, VA 23220
(804) 269-3689
www.saisonrva.com
@SaisonRVA
Seventeen beer taps

Sedona Taphouse
15732 WC Main Street, Westchester Commons, Midlothian, VA 23113
(804) 379-0037
www.sedonataphouse.com
@Sedonataphouse
Fifty beer taps

Sergio's Pizza
4824 Market Square Lane, Midlothian, VA 23112
(804) 744-0111
www.sergiosva.com
@SergiosPizzaVa
Thirty beer taps

Siné Irish Pub & Restaurant
1327 East Cary Street, Richmond, VA 23219
(804) 649-7767
www.sineirishpub.com
@sineirishpubric
Thirty-five beer taps

Southern Railway Taphouse
111 Virginia Street #100, Richmond, VA 23219
(804) 308-8350
www.srtaphouse.com
@SR_Taphouse
Forty beer taps

TJ's Restaurant
The Jefferson Hotel
101 West Franklin Street, Richmond, VA 23220
(804) 649-4750
www.jeffersonhotel.com
@TJs_Restaurant
Eight taps (worth the visit for the elegant setting)

Beer Specialty Shops

(Wine and cider also available.)

The Caboose Wine & Cheese
108 South Railroad Avenue, Ashland, VA 23005
(804) 978-2933
www.facebook.com/pages/The-Caboose-Wine-Cheese/188628038008

Corks & Kegs
7110 Patterson Avenue, Richmond, VA 23229
(804) 288-0816
www.corksandkegs.com
@CorksandKegs

De Fles Winkel
11355 Nuckols Road, Glen Allen, VA 23059
(804) 447-3065
www.defleswinkel.com
@defleswinkel

Ellwood Thompson's
Four North Thompson Street, Richmond, VA 23221
(804) 359-7525
www.ellwoodthompsons.com
@Ellwoods
Specialty grocery with good beer selection

Once Upon a Vine
Two locations
4009 MacArthur Avenue, Richmond, VA 23227
(804) 726-9463
Stratford Hills Shopping Center
2817 Hathaway Road, Richmond, VA 23225
(804) 864-9463
www.onceuponavine.us
@onceuponabeer
Also has limited growler fills

Southern Season
2250 Staples Mill Road, Richmond, VA 23230
(855) 592-3446
www.southernseason.com
@SouthrnSeasnRVA
Specialty grocery with good beer selection

Total Wine & More
Two locations
8099 West Broad Street, Richmond, VA 23294
(804) 935-7750
10036 Robious Road, Richmond, VA 23235
(804) 323-5866
www.totalwine.com
@TotalWineVA

Whole Foods Market
11173 West Broad Street, Richmond, VA 23060
(804) 364-4050
www.wholefoodsmarket.com
@WFMShortPump
Specialty grocery with pints and growler fills from a half-dozen taps

HOMEBREWING RESOURCES

Here are some resources for buying homebrewing supplies or joining fellow
aficionados in the Richmond metro area.

James River Homebrewers
Homebrewing club
www.jrhb.org
Meets the second Wednesday of each month at Mekong Restaurant, 6004
    West Broad Street, Richmond.
Contact Anna Shore at president@jrhb.org. Sponsors the Dominion Cup,
    Virginia's largest homebrew competition, traditionally in August.

Mentoring Advanced Standards of Homebrewing (MASH)
Homebrewing club
www.facebook.com/MASHRVA
Meets the third Thursday of each month, currently at Sergio's Pizza, 4824
    Market Square Lane, Midlothian.
For details, e-mail mashclubrva@gmail.com.

Original Gravity
6920 Lakeside Avenue, Suite D, Richmond, VA 23228
(804) 264-4808
www.oggravity.com
Beer and wine homebrewing supplies

WeekEnd Brewer
4205 West Hundred Road, Chester, VA 23281
(804) 796-9760
www.weekendbrewer.com
@weekendbrewer
Beer and wine homebrewing supplies

In planning: Artisan's Wine and Homebrew
13829 Village Place Drive, Midlothian, VA 23112

Miscellaneous

Blue Bee Cider
212 West Sixth Street, Richmond, VA 23224
(804) 231-0280
www.bluebeecider.com
@BlueBeeCider
Virginia's first urban cidery, offering a variety of ciders, including Hopsap
  Shandy, a hop-infused cider

Richmond Brewery Tours
(804) 404-BREW
www.richmondbrewerytours.com
Guided visits to Richmond breweries, with snacks and refreshments

BIBLIOGRAPHY

BOOKS

Acitelli, Tom. *The Audacity of Hops: The History of America's Craft Beer Revolution.* Chicago: Review Press, 2013.

Blanton, Dr. Wyndham B. *Medicine in Virginia in the Seventeenth Century.* New York: Arno Press, 1972.

Bruce, Philip Alexander. *Economic History of Virginia in the Seventeenth Century: An Inquiry into the Material Condition of the People, Based upon Original and Contemporaneous Records.* New York: McMillan Company, 1935.

Dabney, Virginius. *Richmond: The Story of a City.* Garden City, NY: Doubleday & Company, 1976.

Green, Carol C. *Chimborazo: The Confederacy's Largest Hospital.* Knoxville: University of Tennessee Press, 2004.

Jackson, Michael. *Ultimate Beer.* London: DK Publishing, Inc., 1998.

———. *The World Guide to Beer.* Upper Saddle River, NJ: Prentice-Hall, Inc., 1977.

Kollatz, Harry, Jr. *True Richmond Stories: Historic Tales from Virginia's Capital.* Charleston, SC: The History Press, 2007.

Little, John P. *History of Richmond.* Petersburg, VA: Dietz Press, 1933.

Manarin, Louis H., and Clifford Dowdy. *The History of Henrico County.* Charlottesville: University of Virginia Press, 1985.

BIBLIOGRAPHY

Mehrlander, Andrea. *The Germans of Charleston, Richmond and New Orleans during the Civil War Period, 1850–1870.* Berlin: Walter de Gruyter GmbH & Co., KG, 2011.

Mordecai, Samuel. *Virginia, Especially Richmond, in By-Gone Days.* Richmond, VA: West & Johnson, 1860.

Morris, Danny. *Richmond Beers: A Directory of the Breweries and Bottlers of Richmond, Virginia.* Richmond, VA: Book Printers, 1990. Second edition, with Jeff Johnson. Hong Kong: Colorprint International Ltd., 2000.

Myers, Erik Lars. *North Carolina Craft Beer and Breweries.* Winston-Salem, NC: John F. Blair Publishers, 2012.

Noon, Mark A. *Yuengling: A History of America's Oldest Brewery.* Jefferson, NC: McFarland & Company, 1958.

Ogle, Maureen. *Ambitious Brew: The Story of American Beer.* New York: Harcourt, Inc., 2006.

Oliver, Garrett, ed. *The Oxford Companion to Beer.* Oxford, UK: Oxford University Press, 2012.

Pollard, Julia Cuthbert. *Richmond's Story.* Richmond, VA: Richmond School Board, 2012.

Sanford, James K. *Richmond: Her Triumphs, Tragedies and Growth.* Richmond, VA: Richmond Chamber of Commerce, 1975.

Schuricht, Herrmann. *The History of the German Element in Virginia.* Baltimore, MD: Genealogical Publishing Company, 1977.

Smith, Gregg. *Beer in America: The Early Years (1587–1840).* Boulder, CO: Siris Books, 1998.

Tyler-McGraw, Marie. *At the Falls: Richmond, Virginia and Its People.* Chapel Hill: University of North Carolina Press, 1994.

Ward, Harry M., and Harold E. Greer Jr. *Richmond During the Revolution, 1775–83.* Charlottesville: University of Virginia Press, 1978.

Weisiger, Benjamin B., III. *Old Manchester and Its Environs, 1769–1910.* Richmond, VA: B.B. Weisiger III, 1993.

Wust, Klaus. *The Virginia Germans.* Charlottesville: University Press of Virginia, 1969.

ARTICLES

Distinction. "Beer Reborn." February 17, 2013.

Richmond.com. "More Booze in Richmond—Mead Coming to Scott's Addition." June 10, 2014.

———. "New Business Capitalizes on Craft Beer's Popularity." July 8, 2014.

BIBLIOGRAPHY

Richmond Times-Dispatch. "After a Batch of Brew Comes the Brewery."
September 5, 1982.
————. "Brewery to Skip Chesterfield Site." December 24, 1975.
————. "Called from Church to Save the Day." July 10, 1911.
————. "The Land They Love: Richmond Germans Cherish Fond
Memories of Their Birthplace." October 7, 1890.
————. "Malt, Hops Renew Friendship and City Again Boasts Brewery." 1934.
————. Numerous articles by the author, 1996–2002.
————. "Richmond Brewery Complete." August 29, 1891.
————. "Street Named Fritz Honors Self-Made Man." July 19, 1953.
————. "Virginia Breweries May Divide Product." June 21, 1916.
————. "Wrangling About a Premium." October 26, 1892.
RVA Magazine. "Richmond Beeristoric: A History of Beer Brewing in RVA."
January 24, 2014.
Style Weekly. "State of the Keg." July 29, 2014.
Times (Richmond, VA). "Gambrinus in Richmond." March 3, 1893.
Washington Post. "New Brewery Goes for Gusto." September 25, 1984.

ONLINE SOURCES

Craft Beer Club. "Legend Brewing Company." 2013. http://craftbeerclub.
com/resources/newsletter/Legend-Brewing-Company-VA-1199.
Dennée, Timothy J. "Robert Portner and His Brewing Company." https://
www.alexandriava.gov/uploadedFiles/historic/info/archaeology/
ARSiteReportHistoryPortnerBrewingCoAX196.pdf.
Geocaching.com. "Geocache Historic Brewery Tour of Richmond."
Groundspeak Inc., 2000–13. www.geocaching.com/geocache/
GC2RD0B_historic-brewery-tour-of-richmond-va.
Higgins, Casey. "Virginia's Craft Beer History." http://blog.virginia.
org/2013/08/virginias-craft-beer-history.
Library of Virginia. Out of the Box. "How Dry I Am—The Virginia
Prohibition Commission Records." http://ead.lib.virginia.edu/vivaxtf/
view?docId=lva/vi01055.xml.
Mariners' Museum. Chesapeake Bay: Our History and Our Future.
"Colonial Period: Gabriel Archer." 2002. www.marinersmuseum.org/
sites/micro/cbhf/colonial/col008.html.
Michael Jackson's Beer Hunter. "Flying the Beer Flag on Fourth of July."
www.beerhunter.com/documents/19133-000937.html.

BIBLIOGRAPHY

RustyCans.com. "Krueger Ale." www.rustycans.com/COM/month0406.html.
Schaffer Library of Drug Policy. "History of Alcohol Prohibition." www.druglibrary.org/schaffer.
Thomas Jefferson's Monticello. "Beer." 2014. www.monticello.org/site/research-and-collections/beer#footnotes19_0856401.
———. "Humulus Lupus—Hops." 2010. www.monticello.org/site/plantation-and-slavery/humulus-hops.
University of Virginia Alumni Magazine. "Pioneer of Beer: Charlie Papazian Changed American Brewing Scene." http://uvamagazine.org/articles/pioneer_of_beer.

OTHER SOURCES

Jackson, Jack, comp. *History of the James River Homebrewers*. N.p., 2004.
Smith, J. Douglas. *Wetherburn's Tavern Historical Report, Block 9 Building 13*. 1968.

Note: This book makes use of numerous magazine, newspaper and online articles written by the author, including those published by the *Richmond Times-Dispatch* (as noted previously), *Richmond BizSense*, *Virginia Business Magazine* and *Virginia Golfer Magazine*.

INDEX

INDEX

INDEX

Jefferson, Thomas 5, 15, 18, 22, 75, 129, 150
Jones, Mike and Linda 125
Jones, Scott 99, 100

K

Karns, Paul 101, 102, 103
Kersten, Emil 40, 44, 48
Killelea, Mike 90, 91
Kistler, Devon 129, 130
Kollar, Jim 63
Korol, Jean 78, 79
Kramer, Amy 132
Krueger Brewing Company 56, 58

L

lager 9, 22, 23, 24, 25, 28, 30, 32, 33, 35, 36, 42, 43, 44, 56, 91, 101, 157
Lange, J.G. 24
Lee, Robert E. 28, 29
Legend Brewing Company 65, 76, 84, 107, 138, 149
Leon, Dave 79
Leppert, Tom 64, 65
Levens, Richard 16
Lickinghole Creek Craft Brewery 85, 94, 105, 124, 131, 133, 138
Lincoln, Abraham 29
Lost Rhino Brewing Company 114, 118
Loutfi, Farris 95
Loveland Distributing Company 60, 62, 70, 127

M

Main Street Beer Company 71, 72
Mapp Act 50, 51
Marshall, John 17
Martin, Tom 66, 67, 70, 78, 84, 85, 86
Mayo, John 18
Mayo, William 15
McClenny, Rita 116
McDonnell, Bob 80
McKay, Eric 81, 82, 83, 89, 99, 121, 122

McLellan, Jennifer 80
McWaters, Jeff 80
Mekong Restaurant 8, 10, 79, 109, 110, 123, 124, 126, 141, 145
Mentoring Advanced Standards of Homebrewing 78, 145
Merchants Cold Storage and Ice Company 47
Metz, Jeff 112
Meyer, Ernest 42
Midnight Brewery 87, 103, 138
Miller Brewing Company 63
MillerCoors 116
Mobjack Bay Brewing Company 67, 68, 70, 72
Mordecai, Samuel 17, 18, 24, 148
Mortensen, Brad 107
Mouer, Dan 74
Murtaugh, Patrick 81, 82, 83, 89, 99

N

Nelson, Brian 81
Newport, Christopher 11, 61, 81, 112

O

O'Connor Brewing Company 88
Old Dominion Brewing Company 44, 69
Old Dominion Hops Co-op 118
Old Dominion Mobile Canning 128
O'Leary, Kevin 101
Oliver, Jason 116
Original Gravity 78, 79, 131, 146

P

Pale Fire Brewing Company 114
Papazian, Charlie 62, 72, 75, 78, 79, 150
Parahunt 11
Parkway Brewing Company 114
Peron, Lou 63
Piedmont Hops 118, 129
Poe, Edgar Allan 21, 22, 69
Port City Brewing Company 114, 118

INDEX

INDEX

ABOUT THE AUTHOR

Lee Graves received his baptism into the world of wonderfully diverse beer during a visit to Germany in 1986. From a visit to a monastery where the monks brewed a high-octane schwarzbier to the Hofbrauhaus in Munich, where strangers became friends over brimming liters of lager, he experienced a culture that set him on a lifelong adventure learning about beer. In 1996, while a writer and editor at the *Richmond Times-Dispatch*, he began writing a weekly column about beer; it was syndicated by Tribune Media Services in Chicago for several years. He covered the surge and ebb of craft brewing's first wave of popularity and won several awards as a member of the North American Guild of Beer Writers. A lifelong resident of Virginia and graduate of the College of William and Mary, he continues to write about beer for the *Times-Dispatch* and several magazines, as well as posts on his website, www.leegraves.com. He has spoken frequently to community and professional groups about beer, has taught a beer education class, has kept his hand in homebrewing (he belongs to the James River Homebrewers) and basically bends the ear of anyone who will listen about the incredibly multifaceted universe of beer and the bonds that link those who love it. Graves currently lives in Richmond with his wife, Marggie.